"I love how Kay brings great wisdom to bear on the kind of real life all of us are experiencing. Who's not overwhelmed, right? Here's someone who can guide you to the rest and peace and joy your soul is craving."

Bob Lepine, cohost of *FamilyLife Today*

"I've learned to trust Kay Wyma in matters of family—and life. . . . In *Not the Boss of Us* she shoves the overwhelming threats around us back into the shadows and allows us to embrace the freedom for which Christ set us free."

Elisa Morgan, speaker; author of *The Beauty of Broken* and
The Prayer Coin; cohost of *Discover the Word*;
president emerita of MOPS International

"All of us have times when life feels like a rat race—and the rats are winning! The chaotic pace of modern life can wreak havoc on our health, our families, and our sanity. But Kay Wills Wyma offers an encouraging and uplifting reminder that there's a better way. We don't have to let the tyranny of the urgent rob us of our joy."

Jim Daly, president of Focus on the Family

"Kay has always been the friend who realigns my thinking and reshapes my heart—guiding me gently back to truth every time. This is exactly what she does throughout every page of *Not the Boss of Us*. It's a much-needed mind-set shakeup in a world drowning in overwhelmed."

Courtney DeFeo, author of *In This House,*
We Will Giggle and creator of ABC Scripture Cards

"This book is a breath of fresh air. Kay Wyma's humor, honesty, and insight will inspire and encourage you to make some *very* good trades. Rather than allowing yourself to be overwhelmed by the trappings and pressures that seem chronic in this fast-paced world, Kay will show you how to slow down and lean into your Heavenly Father—who, by the way, made you for so much more."

Sandra Stanley, North Point Ministries

"In *Not the Boss of Us*, Kay doesn't gloss over the complexities of the daily demands we face. Instead she shows us how those demands don't get to dictate how we live. Kay is a gifted storyteller who weaves both compassion *and* invitation into this book that is a must-read for any woman who has ever felt overwhelmed and under pressure. In these pages you will—you can't not—find the freedom-full way of life you've been longing to discover."

Jeannie Cunnion, author of *Mom Set Free*

"I was captivated by the real stories that Kay shares, making the words come alive as she illustrates the importance of us putting our focus on our almighty God—the only real strength for any of us especially when we are overwhelmed. As I interact with women in the workplace, I see so many getting caught up in material trappings, titles, accomplishments, etc. Sometimes God interrupts when our perspective gets out of whack. He did with me. *Not the Boss of Us* is a must-read for everyone."

Diane Paddison, business leader; founder and executive director of 4word; author of *Work, Love, Pray* and *Be Refreshed*

Not the Boss of Us

PUTTING **OVERWHELMED** IN ITS PLACE IN A DO-ALL, BE-ALL WORLD

Kay Wills Wyma

Revell

a division of Baker Publishing Group
Grand Rapids, Michigan

© 2018 by Kay Wills Wyma

Published by Revell
a division of Baker Publishing Group
PO Box 6287, Grand Rapids, MI 49516-6287
www.revellbooks.com

Printed in the United States of America

Library of Congress Cataloging-in-Publication Data
Names: Wyma, Kay Wills, author.
Title: Not the boss of us : putting overwhelmed in its place in a do-all, be-all world
/ Kay Wills Wyma.
Description: Grand Rapids : Baker Publishing Group, 2018. | Includes
bibliographical references.
Identifiers: LCCN 2018007042 | ISBN 9780800734770 (pbk.)
Subjects: LCSH: Mothers—Religious life. | Christian women—Religious life. | Stress
management—Religious aspects—Christianity. | Expectation (Psychology)—
Religious aspects—Christianity.
Classification: LCC BV4529.18 .W96 2018 | DDC 248.8/43—dc23
LC record available at https://lccn.loc.gov/2018007042

The author is represented by the literary agency of Wolgemuth & Associates, Inc.

18   19   20   21   22   23   24   7   6   5   4   3   2   1

For B

Contents

Contents

Introduction

Things in today's culture absolutely overwhelm us.

In my world with five tween/teen kids, Life's Overwhelmed lurks in school halls where grades, test scores, teams, friend groups, and résumé building—either for a college application or a job—threaten to steal joy and peace since *enough* seems ever elusive with regard to all we need to do. Add that to our own stress, pressures, and life's circumstances and we might feel like we're drowning.

So lots of chats about perspective and truth—especially related to identity and self-worth—are had in the kitchen and the car. I might have also, once or twice, been caught yelling out of the car a little reminder about the world's ways. "This stuff is not the boss of you!"

Words that may have anchored a pep talk I recently gave myself.

Like the items that fall out of the car at school pickup and drop-off, just roll with it, I said to myself, repeating the last part for good measure.

Items had rolled out that morning when feet rushed to scramble out of the car—a water bottle, McDonald's Happy Meal toys, a bouncy ball, and a French fry wrapper. The last item, lifted by a gust of wind, flew from the backseat out the door and over the car, making its way like a butterfly to the playground in plain view of all the gluten-free, nonprocessed-food-eating crowd. At least the water bottle wasn't a Coke bottle.

Slightly embarrassed, but business as usual (we are a family of seven—mess comes with the territory), I shrug-smiled at the carpool monitor, cringing that she actually tried to run after the fry wrapper.

The still-in-the-car kids yet to be dropped at the next stop agonized out loud, "Oh my gosh. We're *so* embarrassing."

The kid escaping our flying-litter car while mid-racing to the field to play with his friends yelled back at me, "Don't forget to come to my presentation."

"I won't, sweetheart. You'll do great!" I singsonged back and then mental-noted, *Don't forget*. What I'd give if mental notes were connected to my calendar or some type of electronic reminder. There needs to be an app for that.

Shotgun passenger muttered under her breath, "Yeah, don't forget him like you forgot me."

"Oh, honey, I'm still so sorry about that." I had forgotten her, and she has never let me live it down. Honestly, I don't blame her. "I didn't forget *you*; I just got lost in a crazy day."

She eye-roll-nodded, reassuring me that she knows I love her but is still not going to let me live it down.

I remember doing the same thing to my mom for the time she drove away, accidentally leaving me at Safeway. Between the time my mom had given me a nickel to get something out of the gum machine and the time it had taken her to walk to the car and unload our cart of dinner groceries, I guess she had forgotten I was with her. Off she drove as I stood watching from the store sidewalk, wondering—*Did I really just get left?*

I could have melted into a puddle of poor-me tears. But I didn't because I knew she loved me and would never really forget me.

So rather than wallow, I went straight inside to our friend Sam the produce man, who promptly called my mom, who was already racing back to get me. We lived in a smallish West Texas town where pretty much everyone knew everyone, and the distance between our house and the store was a whopping five minutes. It was safe; I was safe. I actually learned some important life skills that I continue to tap into, even at my old age. But I still tease my mom about forgetting me.

. She had a lot on her plate with four kids and the same pressures to do all and be all, even though looking back, those pressures didn't seem to have the megaphone they do today. In a world with only four channels on the television, phones connected to cords, and adding machines and electric typewriters the closest things to a personal computer, life's pressures and circumstances didn't seem to have the same death grip they have today. But in the moment, the pressures probably felt relentlessly heavy, especially since I'm sure she compared her pressures to those her mother navigated, which absolutely appeared lighter.

I mentally reminded myself of my son's request and determined to be at school, on time, to watch the patriotic presentations alongside the parents who apparently never forget.

Drop-offs proceeded, as did the day. And I remembered to show up for the school presentations. I sat in the back and relished every moment. Then I raced out to the school parking lot, took note of the strange fact that the car door was unlocked, shrugged it off, got in the car, and made it to the next thing—which is where I fought to hear my own pep talk.

Just roll with it, I mentally cheered again as Overwhelmed threatened a sneak attack, since it lurks in the background pretty much all the time.

This time we were at Supercuts trying to cross "haircut" off our list. We were, sadly, in front of people with no semblance of anonymity that might come with being in a car, which only added more layers to the already staggering balancing act to keep it all together—especially when certain announcements automatically (whether supported by fact or not) bring with them judgment, awkward silence, and stares.

"He's got lice," the hair stylist announced as she put down her comb, un-Velcroed the smock, and scooted him from her chair. "I can't cut his hair until the lice are gone."

Roll with it, I repeated to myself. *And smile like there's not a care in the world.* I used the same smile I had put on in the morning carpool lane. "Okay," I quietly replied.

But this was different. She said *lice* twice—in front of everyone, whoever "everyone" was. I felt the teenager within me ready to cry. My thoughts raced, *Everyone saw, and everyone knows that I'm a horrible mother and that we're slobs. Okay, not full-on slobs—but slobs for sure, because that's who has lice, right?*

"Come back when you have taken care of the lice." *Three times—ugh! "Then* I can cut his hair."

The little guy looked at me for reassurance. I'm not sure he fully grasped the meaning of lice, but he knew something was wrong and that he'd just gotten publicly booted.

I hugged him—keeping my head from touching his. Then I picked up our stuff, plastered on a fake-happy smile, and uttered a southern "Thank you so much; we will do that." I was simply scrambling to find some solid footing.

"Bless your heart," a lady said to me as we made our way to the door, pulling her child a little closer as we approached.

Bless my heart?

That's when I knew it was bad. "Bless your heart" might seem nice on the surface, but around here we all know those words pack a punch. They don't mean what they say. No, their intended message is along the lines of "poor thing" or "how pathetic" or even "thank God it's you and not me"—which is how I'm pretty sure she meant it.

The pair shook their heads in feigned sympathy as we walked by on our way out the door. Apparently, they—like we at that moment—didn't know that lice only like clean hair.

So there.

I'm not sure there ever is one, but that was not a good time for the introduction of lice into our lives. There was no room in the inn for another attention grabber. All the circuits were busy. Call back later.

Though I might have wanted to escape all the pressures, I just couldn't let them get the best of me. We simply didn't have time or the margin for Overwhelmed to do what it does—steal. Plus, over the last several years, we've learned a thing or two about putting Overwhelmed in its place.

Lice. I mean really, who cares? So what if I'd lived through a collective thirty-five years of school (you know, counting each kid) as well as my own life, growing up with three siblings, without that exciting diagnosis.

So what if the haircut experience was preceded by an equally unwanted email announcement informing me of "unusual debit card activity." At least now I knew that my purse, which I had frantically searched for and failed to find, wasn't hiding as I had thought. No, not this time. It had been stolen by someone living high on the hog at the DART station and Walmart. My unlocked car door was actually the result of a break-in. A day that began with flying trash and included a detour to the bank in order to stop payment had now crescendoed with the announcement of *lice*. Overwhelmed perched in my head, eager to take over and steal the show.

I said no.

That driver's license picture was horrible anyway, and cards can be replaced. Thank goodness we live in a time when fraud protection exists! And so what if lice had entered the picture? Sure, I was likely to get them since I had put my head next to his head on a pillow the night before so we could read a book. I'd now be able to genuinely commiserate with lice getters, to empathize rather than be scared and ready to run from them. I'd also get to realize how it's not a big deal.

Later, our niece Shelley, who had grown up in the jungles of Bolivia with her missionary family—the same tribe my husband, Jon, had grown up with—stopped by for dinner. We shared the craziness of the day. She chuckled and nonjudgmentally picked up the lice comb from the counter. Then she started picking the little creatures out of lice boy's hair.

"This reminds me so much of home," she said. "The Ese-Ejas [the Indian tribe with whom they had lived] would sit around and get bugs out of each other's hair—and mine." She laughed as she reminisced. "No one thought anything of it—except that it was so nice to sit and chat and help, or even let someone help you."

She thought for a minute more. "I loved those days by the river."

Ah, perspective.

Perspective acts like a cool drink of water. It quenches internal thirst. It helps us breathe. It refuses to give in to all that attempts to steal the joy from life. Perspective helps by reframing today based on real events, not perceived ones.

But perspective can often be hard to find in the midst of the world's demands.

Pressures, stress, and circumstances can skew the picture of reality—whether we're aware of them or not. And they play into Overwhelmed's hands. Silently filling up and overflowing our capacity, sending what would normally be categorized as just a blip into the form of a cyclone, compelling a stronger response than normal. Overwhelmed is great at lingering in the background, humming like an annoying broken appliance, barely noticeable until you just can't take it anymore. Then Overwhelmed can cause something laughable (after the fact) like a lice lesson, or it can cause deeper, internal mismessaging with much more significant outcomes and consequences.

That's when Overwhelmed has gone too far.

It's bad enough when we're adults, but when the reach of Overwhelmed goes younger and younger, it's even worse. As the next chapter reveals, this is where our story really begins—at the unthinkable.

But please don't lose hope or get tripped up by the enormity of this story's beginning. Because it doesn't end there. As in all good stories, a hero stands ready to race in and save the day. This hero is known as Truth, and he stands ready to inform and turn the volume down on the distorted messages and pressures of the world.

And it's at that point that Overwhelmed can be literally transformed from bad to good.

one

The Beginning of the End of Overwhelmed as We Knew It

Life is ten percent what happens to you, ninety percent how you respond.

Lou Holtz

Walking by a hearse with a teenage daughter isn't on my top-ten list of things I'd like to do.

Sitting next to that teenage daughter at the end of a row of her grieving friends, all struggling with disbelief, in a sanctuary anchored by a simple pine casket is not on that list either. Especially when that casket holds the lifeless body of their fourteen-year-old friend.

That was us.

It was real.

The hearse, patiently waiting in the circular drive of the church parking lot, stood at alert, ready to transport the body of my daughter's friend to its final resting place—a grave under cold, hard mounds of dirt.

Never before had the concept of burial felt so heavy.

My daughter got the news about her friend on a Sunday afternoon. We were lazily doing what we love to do, sitting in our living room in front of a cozy fire. With Food Network playing in the background, Barton glanced at her phone at an incoming message. She looked at it.

Then looked at it again.

Put the phone down. Picked the phone up. Looked again.

"What?" she whispered, barely able to access her voice. She fought to find air so she could breathe. Then she said amid disbelief, "B is dead?"

I could barely hear her, but I undeniably felt something heavy coming from where she was sitting. I looked up from my computer. "Honey, what is it?" I asked.

She just shook her head like an Etch A Sketch, trying to erase what had just been drawn so she could grab the knobs and create a different picture. A regular one. The one that had been there before the text.

"I don't know," she said, head still shaking. "I don't know." She hoped it was some sick, bad joke since texts were now flying. If only.

"Honey, talk to me," I gently implored.

She said the words again, this time loud enough to be heard. "B is dead." This proclamation made them real. "She's . . . ," head still shaking, "she's dead." Tears softly joined the conversation, silently adding their response as they made their way from Barton's eyes down her cheeks, cheeks anchoring a mouth that was still fighting to find air.

And with that stomach-turning, unimaginable, gut-wrenching, sorrow-drenched utterance, my daughter (and all of us) began a journey down a road paved with whats, hows, and whys in a battle to make sense of it all.

Two days later, we sat next to each other in a packed sanctuary of people gathered to pay last respects in honor of a life cut desperately short. I looked at the girls who filled our row. My heart ached at the deep confusion, sorrow, and disbelief clouding their countenances. None of this made sense. The entire situation seemed surreal.

B's decision shocked everyone. Shock is an understatement. Her friend group was as encouraging and others-centered as any can be at their age. She had been arguably the most encouraging and others centered of the crew—inspiring these qualities in her friends. She had had a genuinely loving and communicative family, a committed community of faith, a lineup of supportive teachers.

What had she been thinking?

What lies had stolen her thoughts?

Apparently, somewhere deep inside, discouragement, inadequacy, and never-ending pressures to measure up, to be all, and to do all had duped this sweet girl into believing that her self-worth was tethered to something other than Truth. Identity and self-worth had anchored themselves to perpetual motion and elusive measuring marks. And it had been too much. We'll never know exactly which lie won, because we can't ask her. And no one knew she needed to be asked—deeper, more seriously than she had been. She had been so busy encouraging everyone else, making those around her smile, that it had been easy to assume her tank was filled.

But in a place only she knew, her tank was completely empty, dry. And she is so very missed.

It wasn't cancer. It wasn't physical illness. It wasn't a car wreck or a drive-by shooting. No, in large part life pressures and the perceived inability to live in the midst of them shattered that January day. Was depression at play? Possibly. Likely, in fact. But depression's favorite friends—anxiety, fear, loneliness, negative self-view, and the like—find all sorts of traction in Life's Overwhelmed and its silent onslaught and hidden traps that can act as lighter fluid on glowing embers.

19

Though the situation was without a doubt extreme, it certainly shined a bright light on the devastation that comes with Overwhelmed. In this case, it contributed to death. In every case, it saps life. Usually not all of it. But pieces of our lives are stripped away.

We can't bring B back, but we can take something horrible and try to find good on the other side. It's what B would have wanted. She never desired for anyone to feel left out, alone, unloved, or desperate. In fact, just the opposite.

In the aftermath of devastation, a battle cry has gone out and a line has been drawn in the sand, at least in our house. We're sick of Overwhelmed. Tired of it weighing down the people with whom we live life. Tired of life labeling people, then duping them into thinking that all is okay only if or when. Worn out by the stress bombs that steal life and replace it with scrambling at best—isolation at worst.

We say no more to stress-induced, pressure-laden Overwhelmed. It is not the boss of us. Every aspect of Overwhelmed—the big, the small, and all its sneaky attempts to steal peace and joy— has been put on notice.

This particular story about Overwhelmed begins at a funeral, but it doesn't end there. It doesn't have to end there because Truth and hope are present to diffuse the often overwhelming nature of the world's seemingly endless iterations of formulaic right ways to live.

Though Truth and hope can be hard to see in the midst of it all, we can find them. Because we don't have to rely solely on ourselves. Maybe that's a part of why we're not alone on this earth. I mean, if we were supposed to travel life's journey by ourselves, God would have made it that way.

So in an effort to walk alongside, to call out what threatens so many of our days, and to encourage looking for the light and for life, this story shares a little about our trek. It's a road paved with laughter and with tears. And since no one need laugh or cry alone, it's a road to be traveled together.

Together, knowing no one is alone, we can call out Life's

Overwhelmed in order to avoid and turn down the volume on messages that claim to be, but couldn't be farther from, the truth.

Calling Out and Reframing Life's Overwhelmed

We probably need to begin this journey by putting some structure to a nebulous and undeniably spiritual subject. The word *Overwhelmed* itself is overwhelming. And soul topics are ambiguous, taking clear-cut and throwing it out the window. Which might be why it's so hard to get our arms around it. But just because something is hard to address, doesn't mean it can't be. And since Overwhelmed is powerful, it must be.

What is Overwhelmed?

According to Merriam-Webster, *overwhelm* is a transitive verb meaning: (1) to upset, overthrow; (2) to cover over completely, submerge; (3) to overpower in thought or feeling.[1]

And we do feel it. Life's Overwhelmed can look like anxiety as endless iterations of what-ifs capture our thoughts and accompany societal messaging that you're-only-okay-if:

- You are in a certain group or profession
- You have achieved certain pinnacles (athletic, academic, professional, etc.)
- You attend certain schools
- You look a certain way or wear a certain size
- You have a powerhouse résumé
- And so much more

Life's Overwhelmed floods our thoughts with fear that we're not-okay-because:

- You are struggling
- Your kid is struggling (since we've been convinced that our child's success or failure is a reflection of our parenting skills)

21

- You weren't invited
- Your kid isn't invited
- You were passed over for a promotion
- Your kid is passed over for the team or position or role
- Your calendar is too empty
- Your calendar is too full
- You feel alone
- Your kid is alone
- Unexpected life-twists and turns
- Sickness or death (not only physical but relational as well)
- And so much more

Recently, "a mail carrier in Brooklyn stashed about 17,000 pieces of undelivered mail for more than a decade because he was 'overwhelmed' by the amount he had to deliver." He told authorities that he did deliver the "important" mail before being charged.[2] Honestly, he might have been a help to all of us who feel overwhelmed by the amount of mail we get—mostly junk. Like lots of things in life, finding what's real within the junk can be a challenge.

Getting our hands on a topic like Life's Overwhelmed feels like trying to lasso a cloud. So, I'm sure we'll all have frustration along the way. Especially since this effort's tour guide happens to be on the tour too. Not only has it hurt people for whom I deeply care, it also wields entirely too much power.

Since we've called out and started to reframe Overwhelmed around our house, we've tasted some significant freedom. We've started to realize that Overwhelmed goes two ways and is undeniably more powerful when attached to Truth—with all of its grace, peace, hope, and love. By opting to be overwhelmed by Truth instead of the culture's stress and pressures, we get hit with blasts of oxygen rather than pulled down by feelings of drowning.

We may never be rid of life's pressures and challenging circumstances that play lead roles in Overwhelmed's plan of attack, but there's joy in the midst.

Pressures tend to rely heavily on messaging as well as mismessaging. They have always existed and will continue to exist. Mismessaging hardwires itself into our thoughts, especially when we're kids. Young people haven't had the luxury or the time or the money to hone wall-building or layer-laying skills that adults use to cope, stuff, insulate, and conceal—otherwise known as an effort to control. The world around them—with its instant-imaging, social media, anonymity-based platforms—can pack plenty of punch, making a fit kid feel fat and a smart kid feel stupid. It can make almost anyone feel completely alone while sitting in a crowd.

Sound familiar?

Mismessaging doesn't limit itself to kids. We all tend to be a flesh wound away from junior high insecurities, which might be why Life's Overwhelmed so easily uses life's stresses, pressures, and circumstances like a shoehorn to fit a pair of custom-made concrete boots on a crowd of well-intentioned, just-trying-to-live-life people.

Overwhelmed in and of itself is actually a result rather than an issue. In order to deal with it, we have to dig a little deeper to find the source of what invites Overwhelmed into the conversation.

For the purposes of our effort to put Overwhelmed in its place, we will label the world's pressures, stresses, expectations, hard circumstances, etc., as *Life's Overwhelmed* and its powerful antidote as *Truth*. Truth stands on an age-old reality that often gets overlooked when Life's Overwhelmed feels like rising waters ready to drown us. The wonderful thing about Truth—as soon as it begins to reinform a moment, oxygen fills the air and not only can we breathe easier but peace and hope and joy come along for the ride.

Practically speaking, what does reframing Life's Overwhelmed look like? Let's consider one of the biggest thieves facing a massive portion of society today: performance manifested in the need to hit certain measuring marks in order to be okay. Though the pressures are real, the root source of its message is far from solid. Truth be told, performance measuring marks are in a constant state of flux, making them hard to hit and especially hard to land as they, with absolute certainty, change. So rather than buy into and be overwhelmed by performance pressures, why not instead be overwhelmed by purpose and gifting: in-born traits that are unique to each person and make us happy regardless of what culture celebrates at any given moment. Then live today's day, respecting tomorrow but not allowing fears of it to steal our time and thoughts.

But is choosing to be overwhelmed by Truth real? And how is it possible? Especially since we're led to believe that we're only okay if our kid makes the honor roll, we make certain teams, get a certain job or promotion, wear a certain size of clothing, live in a certain neighborhood, etc. What if those have little to do with what actually makes us okay? Could we choose Truth over pervasive societal messaging?

Why not ponder it together?

If we're willing to address the root issues—the motivators, the messages, and the drivers—we might be able to reach for a refreshing "drink of water" informed by Truth. We just might be able to slow down the absorption of societal messaging and be overwhelmed by perspective messaging—free to live rather than be beaten down or discouraged.

Though kids live out loud and can tend to be raw—at least for a little while—once they're unheard, misheard, or unnoticed, they can shut down or even give in to rewiring. Then they may actually believe negative messaging rather than find grounding in things that are true—like their inherent worth, giftedness, and purpose. Something that is absolutely true for adults too.

That's where reframing or even repurposing can come into play. Why not call out Life's Overwhelmed, address the spots where it

A Teacher's Email to Parents:

YOU'RE NOT ALONE

It appears that we have begun the year successfully, though I wanted to share with you about our experience this morning. As class began, I asked the students how many of them were feeling overwhelmed or stressed. Nearly the entire class raised their hands. I asked them to look around the room and notice that they are not alone. I told them that we are often tricked into thinking we are the only one feeling that way, but in fact many are experiencing stress during this transition into middle school. I am sure many of you as parents are feeling the same way. Please be encouraged—this is a normal experience in Class Five, and I want to be able to help your family any way I can.

Mrs. Emmanuel,
5th grade teacher

resides, and flip it to good? Who knows—maybe calling it out for our kids and friends can, in turn, inform us.

Which is usually the case around here. I almost always need to hear whatever I'm telling my kids. And core things haven't changed much since I was in high school or college or the workforce or different stages of parenting. I'm guessing they will be the same when I'm grandparenting.

So rather than be overwhelmed by—

- performance pressures that bring with them persona pressures of the be-all variety;
- do-all pressures that constantly beg for more—as if filled spaces inform our importance and worth;
- ahead pressures—as in getting, staying, or finishing ahead, even in places as regular as the cafeteria line or roadway—and the insensitivities that come with them;

- formulaic right-way pressures and religion—not faith but religion, with all the tasks and rituals required in order to be okay;
- information overload—local, national, and international news;
- technology—not only the ever-shifting environment but also the unknowns and the evils;
- people and relationship issues with all their complexities and minefields of misunderstanding;
- an overload of choices and expectations;
- life circumstances that prompt fear, worry, sadness, frustration, or jealousy; and
- simply the sheer volume of stuff

—why not be overwhelmed by Truth?

Rather than be waylaid by Life's Overwhelmed, let's be filled to overflowing with Truth's hope and grace and love and peace. Rather than compare or compete against people, let's walk alongside them. Because the common denominator and the part of the picture that often gets blurred in Life's Overwhelmed are actually what matter most: people—others as well as ourselves. Yes, ourselves. Though hardest to admit or believe, we matter and have significant worth.

Rather than wait until the fires of Life's Overwhelmed are blazing, why not take practical steps today and practice drowning out life's pressures so that we will already be accustomed to saying no when heat rises? We need to let our actions act like a cool drink of water so that we're fully hydrated—constantly being overwhelmed by Truth rather than caving to overwhelming issues of the world.

If we were planning to run a marathon, we would prepare our bodies for what's coming by hydrating (not to mention months of training). Because, as athletes know, by the time you feel thirsty, it's too late. Why not apply the same rules to soul hydration? With all of life's rushing and keeping up and coordinating and doing and so much more, the soul can get dangerously depleted and emptied.

But hydration is not a quick fix.

I'm a fellow sojourner, seeking and testing the path because around here, we're sick of the world's all-inclusive resort that feeds everything but the soul. I am a wife and a mom, so a lot of our story stems from this life stage and occupation—even though Overwhelmed most certainly shows up in all stages of life and every occupation.

Our story involves the people closest to me, including my kids—whom I not only love but genuinely like a lot—whose stories are not mine but yet are. Years ago, another story involved them. We were as tired of entitlement then as we are tired of Overwhelmed now. And since these kind people who travel life next to me prefer anonymity, we gave them aliases. Bear with the fake identities—we have naming issues over here. In fact, we left the hospital on multiple occasions without naming our kids. Yes, you can leave with "Baby" on the birth certificate—for several weeks.

So here you go:

- Boxster. A young man of deep character, named after a memorable conversation involving a Porsche and teen-induced car envy long since past.
- Snopes. Named for her keen ability to see beyond the surface to truth that often lies below.
- Barton. After the great Clara Barton, who was quick to assess a situation and step in to help and manage, even on a battlefield.
- Fury. Named after one of my favorite childhood reads, he's a passionate, gritty kid who's willing to take the road less traveled.
- And Birdie. As in *a little birdie told me*, since many of the things he tells me involve the unassuming yet profound wisdom of a child worth remembering.

27

"Do you know why we can't see tomorrow?" Birdie recently asked then answered himself. "Because we can only live today."

Truth. Truth that tomorrow's worries and yesterday's happenings don't get to overinform or steal from today.

I hope what is shared within these pages helps dial down Life's Overwhelmed. Up to this point, choosing to be overwhelmed by Truth has, more than anything, shown us that we're not alone. And that hope absolutely abounds along with her good friend freedom

Sound a bit eye-roll worthy? Maybe. But it works. Truth is funny that way, and nothing is lost in trying. You never know what might happen with Life's Overwhelmed reframed. Because, the truth is, it's just not the boss of us.

Person not Persona

For kids, many of life's stresses find life in the performance-pressure vise grip that dupes them into believing they have to achieve, be, and do in order to be okay. People feel compelled to create and put forth a persona that appears put together, cool, and in control when who knows what's going on beneath the surface. Measuring lines involving all things GPA or SAT or varsity or the right invitation or car or date or clothes or the right group are nothing short of ruthless. The minute a measuring line is within reach, it moves and demands more. Overwhelming.

Overwhelmed is an equal opportunity invader. We all feel it, fight it, and try to overcome it. Like a shapeshifter, it morphs into different forms at different life stages: marriage/no marriage, kids/no kids, fitness, education, job, finances, responsibilities, aging parents, retirement, politics . . . is there an end?

If this were a physical problem, scientists and pharmaceutical companies would be on it.

per · son · a /pər'sō-nə/ *noun*
The public image you present to the world. In ancient Latin, the word *persona* meant "mask."[3]

28

Researching, experimenting, and concocting. Commercials with fast-talking disclaimers would fill the airwaves. But the things that drive Overwhelmed tend to live in the soul.

And soul topics require time and pondering with open and honest dialogue, seasoned with love and light on judgment. Soul topics need a steady flow of fresh oxygen and hydration in order for us to refocus and gain proper perspective.

So on that particularly hard day when news of sadness filled a phone screen, that's where my daughter and I started, with time—much of it quiet—and with honest talk perched on the sideline like a water station waiting and ready to gently enter and offer a cool drink to wounded souls.

Talking—that simple, commonplace activity that we usually take for granted—is critically important. And one of the greatest opportunities that comes with talking is listening. Talking and listening, but not in a prescribed way. The truth is, if each party is willing to listen, we all have something to gain.

That day, Barton and I talked about how hard life can be—we don't have to pretend like it isn't. We talked about seeing the unseen—how we all need help to keep our eyes open to see beyond ourselves, to see the lonely, to see the sad, to see the good when someone can't see it themselves. We talked about compassion—the importance of considering how someone else feels when _____ (blank) happens. We talked about how there is more to life than a moment and that self-worth isn't determined by a score or a grade or a party invitation. And we talked about fear.

We searched for and called out reminders founded in perspective—from my own life (you know, looking back it wasn't such a big deal that I spent most of my Saturday nights with Julie and her *Love Boat* crew) and from hers (looking back she sees a first- grade playground-takedown not as a blight but as an introduction to compassion through empathy). Perspective is always available. It tends to bring with it some needed oxygen.

And we talked about how life goes on—and that's okay. Smiles, laughter, happiness, joy are still there. It's good for life to go on.

I'm not naïve enough to think that talking will solve everything, but it's a big start. And maybe while we're talking, we can get to the place where Truth breaks through, the truth that we all—at the core of our being—desire to be known, to be loved, and to belong. And maybe through talking and listening, we can cross the chasm.

What I'd give for Barton's friend who listened to and acted on the extreme lie that the world would be better off without her to have instead heard the truth that she is a person who is loved, who absolutely belonged, and who is missed.

Curious, I asked our other daughter, Snopes, what she thought. Are these desires—to be known, to be loved, to belong—at our core? Are they the drivers that need addressing and a jolt of perspective?

Her reply? Yes—on the knowing we're loved part especially.

"Sometimes I catch myself watching a romantic movie and thinking, 'Oh, if only a cute boy would love me that way, then everything would be okay.' Then I remember how loved I am by God, who sacrificed a lot in order to be sure I know. And I want my thoughts anchored in that rather than in all the other stuff around me."

Here's the deal. We often cannot change the environment around us with all its quick-assess, positioning, and you're-only-okay-if pressures. But we do have a voice on its impact. We can change

To be loved but not known is comforting but superficial.

To be known and not loved is our greatest fear.

But to be fully known and truly loved is, well, a lot like being loved by God. It is what we need more than anything. It liberates us from pretense, humbles us out of our self-righteousness, and fortifies us for any difficulty life can throw at us.

Tim Keller[4]

how we act and react within the environment. Which is huge in our effort to tame Overwhelmed.

Actions and Reactions

When I was in high school, I dipped my toe then dove into the inviting waters of an eating disorder. It started with a skinny girl on a diet, as if any teen girl should be on a diet, and ended at full-blown self-destruction mode.

By the time I was a junior in college, I looked up one day and found myself in dire need of help. Asking for help wasn't hard. But there were parts of the help that *were* hard—like actually getting it—and, for me, coming to grips with my faith and the role it had played and could play in my life. Because, how could my claimed faith in God and redemption ever be informing a life that literally wallowed in performance and outward appearance pressures.

I needed the not-alone part of getting into a program for help. I learned so much by sitting in group counseling with a drug addict, a teenage prostitute, a middle-aged morbidly obese man, an obese shopaholic older woman, and a fourteen-year-old anorexic who was my roommate. From the outside, we were a gathering of misfits. From the inside, we were all alike.

All of us had been reaching for self-destructive methods to cope with the pressures in our very different lives—our striving, our circumstances, our need to be known, to belong, and to be loved, really, just to be okay. Our environments clearly differed from each other, yet it amazed me how similar we all were. It still does.

So when the concept of faith entered the picture—as it does in most recovery programs—I had a hard time accepting that putting my faith in a higher power, even in an object like a chair (the example presented to us since it really didn't matter what it was as long as we could get our eyes off ourselves), was the answer.

"I don't think the chair is going to cut it," I announced after taking a deep breath. "I get the needing faith part. And I understand that the higher power can be pictured in our minds as that chair. But I have to say out loud that I'm pretty sure God is the One who can fix this."

I was scared of the rejection that I expected to hit me on the other side of those words, which it did. "If God is your answer," the very kind obese man lobbed back to me—he had been hurt by religion and rejected by people of faith—"why are you here?"

Most of them nodded in agreement.

He was right. It was a question I had asked myself so many times. And, at that point, I didn't know the answer.

"I don't know," I told him. "I think my being here probably has more to do with me and my messed-up understanding of all the things I've believed I have to do in order to be okay than it does with God. But I just don't know. Still, I'm betting on God."

I figured my understanding (whether I could or couldn't) didn't change God. So, I might have felt foolish in front of them, but I held on to the hem and hoped for answers.

I had been so overwhelmed by the doing and being by that point in my life—especially when it came to religion—I literally had to check out in order to stay alive. Eating disorders are still high on the list of coping mechanisms, though cutting and other self-inflicted harm seem to have taken over the spotlight these days. Drugs, alcohol, and the bizarre—like a current trend to consume laundry detergent pods—play their role in numbing people from all that overwhelms. Each method is destructive. None of them give life as advertised.

Little did I know the door to freedom and being overwhelmed by Truth was just on the other side of the hill. But traveling the road isn't easy or instant—which probably has something to do with our propensity to learn by experiencing.

Upon completing that program and getting my feet on some solid ground, the door literally hit me on the way out. I had worked hard to be okay with eating and with accepting myself as who I am, not who I saw or wanted myself to be or even felt like others expected me to be—but my legs were shaky.

I ran into someone very close to me when I got home. "Oh my word, Kay," she said, "are you alright?"

When I left college, I didn't sneak out. I told people. I made an announcement at my sorority meeting, told my teachers, told my friends and even the school leadership since I was junior class treasurer. I didn't want to hide anything. I was done with hiding and wanted nothing more to do with pretense or façades. It's taboo to talk about stuff so intimate and painful, but tabooing a topic results in deeper isolation and so much more pain than airing it out could cause. So when this dear person crossed my path, she knew where I had been and what I had been up to.

"Wow, I'm so glad you've got that behind you," she said. And then she added, "You're home now and can get back to normal. Your pants look a little tight. It will be nice to be able to start eating what you want again."

I had no response. But I smiled through racing thoughts.

Did she really just say that? My pants look tight? Does she know that I can hear her? Could my pants maybe be tight because they're the wrong *size!?—as in too small for me since before getting help I hadn't eaten like a regular person in years!*

I remember it like it was yesterday. I felt the ground shake and start to swallow me—as if all my efforts were for nothing. I would be forever a prisoner to body image, to performance and measurement pressures, feeling like I wasn't good enough. I knew freedom could never be within *my* reach. Maybe for others, but not me.

Right then and there, I mentally screamed at all those tempting thoughts, "No!" I didn't know how, but I knew I had to say no and that I was worth shouting no to it all. Worth is something I'm not sure I had believed about myself before. I might not have used the words, I certainly had heard my parents and teachers shower them over me, but it was probably the first time I fought to grab self-worth. And, though not audibly, I told those messages they were absolutely not the boss of me.

At that point in life, I had only an inkling of an idea about the source of my worth. But I knew placing that fragile self-worth in something like my pant size, or so many other things that begged to claim my identity, was the farthest place from safe.

Standing next to someone who loved me, who I believe said those words out of love since she knew how hard it had all been, I recognized that though I could not change my environment, I could change the way I act in it and react to it.

Words that tried to fast-track me back into bondage—*"Your pants look a little tight"* (a.k.a. you're fat)—needed to take on a different translation. *"I'm trying to commiserate and help, I just don't know how."* It would take some time, but I told myself that from that day forward, I needed to learn how to fully function in rather than expect change from my daily environments. It wasn't going to change, I needed to change. I was not a victim—and apparently never had been, even though I gave environments and the messages woven within them a lot of power to determine my worth.

I'm so grateful for that day. A powerful tool found a place in my pack. A tool that has helped me walk through rather than run from situations. It even helped me love, genuinely love, the people who lived in, and sometimes created, stress-filled environments. I began to feel compassion rather than give way to feelings of judgment or shame.

I've never forgotten that conversation and the power of saying no to mismessaging. I use it often. I share it with my kids. I find myself circling back with the question, "What did you hear me [or your teacher or your coach or whoever] say?" So often Truth can inform our mind-sight that is rarely 20/20. And freedom replaces burden.

The only difference between my mind-set today and that day over thirty years ago is that I understand on a much deeper level where my self-worth and identity are based. And I deeply understand that these environments that tempt to trap our thoughts have nothing on us.

So since environments don't change and we are the ones who have to change the way we interact with them, why not do it together?

Rather than wearing the Super Girl do-all, be-all cape that acts like a duct-tape fix so we can keep going, let's choose some other clothes to wear. Let's dress for an adventure best traveled together on a road paved with authenticity. Maybe then we can openly contemplate underlying issues of insecurity and doubt, of significance and identity. Which is where Truth stands center stage, a place it's been all along.

And as far as things like lice are concerned, we've lived through it, survived it. I recently noticed the bottle of Lice Defense Shampoo that still sits in the shower next to the regular shampoo, and I'm not sure I ever want to move it. I actually love the at-least-we-don't-have-lice reminder. I also love the reminder to be overwhelmed by Truth—that we survived, that there's perspective in the midst, and that the things that attempt to trip us up, though seemingly huge in the moment, are doable.

All of which might have everything to do with people rather than with circumstances.

The Meaning of Life—Love, People, Together

"What's the meaning of life?"

The question floated my way from the backseat. It was lobbed at me by my sole passenger, Birdie, whom I had just retrieved from a birthday party at Lil' Ninjas. He was eight at the time. I thought he was being silly.

"What do you think the meaning of life is?" I tossed back with a little wink in the rearview mirror.

"I don't know," he replied. "That's why I asked you."

35

Oh. He was serious. Apparently, he really wanted an answer. I thought for a minute.

You never know when a deep question—one of those that have floated throughout the ages—will be asked from the backseat of an SUV. I might have sighed an audible "Hmm . . ." as I considered the best way to answer such a grand question from a little kid who apparently thinks big thoughts.

How do you answer a question like that? For an eight-year-old? For yourself? I wondered if it could be boiled down to a simple statement that would satisfy the curiosity of a child or the curiosity of the adult to whom the question had been asked.

Though my thoughts raced through explanations and considered philosophers, theologians, and deep thinkers who had crossed my path, they kept traveling back to love. To love, and to people. Because it seemed to me that God started it all—this place called Earth peppered with good and bad from almost the get-go—as a mysterious outflow of love.

But before I could try to say out loud what I thought about the meaning of life, Birdie gave his opinion.

"I think I know," he began after his own careful contemplation of the question he had asked. "I think the meaning of life is fun."

Hmm . . .

"Okay." I nodded. Then I prodded, "What is fun to you?"

"Well." He paused, possibly running through his own mental reasoning to see if his conclusion rang true. Then he confidently replied, "Fun is spending time with cousins."

His conclusion was the closest thing to a definition of love this side of heaven. When he's with his cousins, he belongs. He is known. There is a nonnegotiable, nonrefundable, undeniable DNA blood relationship. When he's with his cousins, he

> And now these three remain: faith, hope and love. But the greatest of these is love.
>
> 1 Corinthians 13:13

can barely contain the love he feels for them and the happiness he experiences when he's with them—even when the wrestling goes too far. Maybe because they're still around after a fight.

Love and people.

"Yes," he continued. "Cousins and Hawaiian Falls."

"Hawaiian Falls?"

"You know, what's that thing that goes around the water park where you float?" he asked, needing help to find the right words.

"The lazy river?" I offered.

"Yes, the lazy river. It moves you along without you having to try. Yeah—that and cousins is what's fun. And I think that's the meaning of life."

Well, there you have it. The meaning of life. Love. People. Being carried along. Living life alongside. Not on our own strength.

His might not have, but my thoughts instantly traveled to theological significance. The picture of that lazy river in my mind and the people traveling alongside sure had me thinking. As did the power source that moves the lazy river. What if the source is the One who is love, the One who loves the people in the picture, the One who first loved us?

Nothing in Birdie's meaning of life felt overwhelming. Instead, his idea felt infused with peace and fullness.

It felt meaningful.

Real.

Is it possible to be overwhelmed by those things rather than by the pressures and stresses that lead us to believe that life's meaning finds footing in more, best, success, achievements, notoriety, or the number of likes or friends or shares we have?

I think yes.

People, not personas, matter.

Water Station

TALK ABOUT TABOO

"It's taboo. You just can't talk about it," said one of Barton's friends. She was referring to all the things that can't be spoken aloud: failing, wounds, anxieties, fears. It's hard for them, knowing that B had things to say but didn't and somehow thought she couldn't.

Taboo is brutal, overwhelming by the nature of its inherent locked-tight secrecy that finds life in shame. The longer it's locked, the heavier the burden, the larger the issue, the louder the self-messaging.

Taboo-laced shame comes in all shapes and sizes and can live in the distant as well as the recent past. Self-misgivings find basis in minor missteps, mis-met expectations, and judgment (perceived as well as actual), but also in monumentally bad incidents, even when the bad thing is done to us.

Taboo promotes isolation and fools us into thinking we need to hide rather than invite others in. But Taboo doesn't get to win. Taboo is not the boss. *Talk* trumps Taboo.

Brené Brown has this to say:

And I've come to the belief—this is my twelfth year doing this research—that vulnerability is our most accurate measurement of courage—to be . . . vulnerable, to let ourselves be seen, to be honest.

The second thing I learned, is this: We have to talk about shame. . . . Shame is an epidemic in our culture. And to get out from underneath it—to find our way back to each other, we have to understand how it affects us and how it affects the way we're parenting, the way we're working, the way we're looking at each other. . . .

If we're going to find our way back to each other, we have to understand and know empathy, because empathy's the antidote to shame. If you put shame in a Petri dish, it needs three things to grow exponentially: secrecy, silence and judgment. If you put the same amount in a Petri dish and douse it with empathy, it can't survive. The two most powerful words when we're in struggle: me too.[5]

"No taboo for you," the girls agree. "No matter what's going on." Safe-place friends—to have and to be—take a lot of trust, but they are worth the risk.

Talk about Taboo

Say it out loud to someone who genuinely cares. Talking takes Taboo and brings it into the light where perspective and empathy can help reframe and possibly confirm—*me too*; *we're not alone.*

two

Rather Than Be Overwhelmed by Performance Pressures, Be Overwhelmed by Purpose

I am careful not to confuse excellence with perfection. Excellence, I can reach for; perfection is God's business.

Michael J. Fox

Snopes started to scrape the bottom the other night.

My heart literally ached as I stood in the tiny bathroom that she shares with her sister. I had been passing by on my way to bed when I heard soft crying—you know, the slow leak kind. I didn't know if she was missing someone she loved who had recently lost a battle to cancer or if her heart had been hurt by one of the many varieties of fitting in (social media, inclusion, attire, size) that line her walk in life. Those things we think we left behind in junior high but ever linger.

I might have been a bit sensitive to an emotional kid; any upswing of emotions received a little extra scrutiny after B's passing.

I was definitely on heightened awareness—ready to stop any pressure overload and reframe Overwhelmed in its tracks.

I think that's what we do after becoming aware of an issue, especially those involving kids. Mother lion crouches, ready to obliterate anything messing with her cubs. But she doesn't stop there. The circle widens from just her kids to her friends, to other moms at back-to-school sign-ups, to sideline spectators, and to strangers in line at Starbucks perusing Instagram or Facebook. *Hey! That stuff doesn't define you as a person!* I'm clearly done with Life's Overwhelmed messing with anyone traveling through life next to me.

"What's wrong, honey?" I asked, quietly praying that Snopes would open up to me. You never know.

"Nothing."

I gently pushed. Quiet tears aren't like drama tears. They're real and deep. I wanted to know. I needed to know. And I really wanted to nab whatever had grabbed her thoughts and was holding her captive.

Finally, she sighed. The floodgates opened and "I can't do this" burst from her lips.

"This"—not to be dramatic—signified everything in her world. Regular life had been crowded out by a list of roles and demands: social standing, GPA, friend group, filled calendar, athletics, volunteering. When molded together, they create a product, not a life. What you do and where you land determine who you are, whether you are a teenager or a middle-ager. The pressures to be are heavy and incessant.

Mid-sob, sweet Snopes released the horrible admission that threatened to be true if spoken aloud: "I can't be perfect."

The quiet tears briefly morphed into a deep, guttural sob.

When I was her age, normal life included propriety, respect, decorum, and regular, which didn't mean everyone needed to be best. In today's society, normal looks a lot like perfection.

The idea that life is played out as if on a stage is no longer the case. Now life is an always-on, photo-ready, photoshopped reality—anytime, anywhere, even when alone. The audience is always watching. And the bar for success is set at an impossible height, where it stays just out of reach.

But oddly enough, the only thing that gives life to "perfect" is the idea of it. Perfection isn't real. Neither are so many of the other marks set on a variety of self-worth-defining achievement scales.

These standard-setting marks rarely travel alone. They bring an entourage that acts more like thieves than companions. They threaten to steal precious time, bogging us down with worries and fears and pressures that cloud any ability to truly relish the moments and the people around us.

Curious, I decided to ask Siri—I mean, why not—"Is anyone or anything perfect?"

Siri's answer was a lame "Interesting question, Master Overlord." A response that led me to wonder which one of my kids told Siri to call me Master Overlord. The best answer I could find simply said: It depends on what your definition of perfect is.[1] Except in objective, quantifiable cases, such as a multiple-choice exam, perfect is subjective—a far cry from achievable aspirations.

A friend and I recently interviewed Shauna Niequist about the topic. It's something she has deeply explored and contemplated, compiling her assessment in the bestselling *Present over Perfect*. Her take: "I think we can never overestimate how strong the cultural messaging toward perfectionism is. . . . Culture is screaming that message in a loud, one-note way."[2]

Performance pressures, with all their perfection issues, can be overwhelming.

So how do we deal with them?

People are a large part of the answer—as in healthy relationships with the people around us and with ourselves. "You don't have to wake up every morning and perform in order to be loved," Shauna shared.[3]

But for some reason, we find that hard to believe. Probably because almost everything around us sends a message that love and acceptance arrive only when we're good or have done enough to warrant their arrival. So much of belonging and acceptance appears tied to positive performance—that can include grades, a promotion, or even diet and exercise. Striving for a perfect appearance can be a dangerous treadmill leading to nowhere—except to frustration at best, self-harm at worst.

I stood next to my daughter in that tiny bathroom and started down a road I find myself traveling often, a road paved with these words that I now feel as if I'm saying ad nauseam: "I don't know what is stealing your self-worth, but it's not real. Whatever has tricked you into thinking you're okay only if certain things are true is telling you a lie. None of those things define you. Measuring marks change constantly. And your self-worth, *you*, who you are isn't tethered to things that move all the time."

No comment, but listening, which is so much better than being ignored or experiencing a slammed door.

"I'm telling you that the things that act *so* important today will be gone, likely forgotten, and completely different tomorrow. They are not the boss of us."

Whatever is stealing headlines and attention just won't be tomorrow. Case in point:

- In the late 1980s when the time came to sign up for classes— especially to fulfill a language requirement—people fell over themselves to take Japanese. It was the must-speak language, since Japan appeared to be poised for sustained world dominance at that time. Learning Japanese was the golden ticket to success.

- In 1990, when I was beginning my career, a company by the name of KKR (Kohlberg Kravis Roberts) held the headlines and graced the cover of most major business magazines all over the world. Almost all of my business school friends wanted to work for it and companies weren't ashamed to be gobbled up by it. Not only was this company an industry leader but its name was also almost synonymous with the LBO (Leveraged Buyout) trend itself. Your name on its business card meant something.
- In 2005, the SAT or Scholastic Achievement Test changed from a maximum 1600 points to 2400 points, largely through the addition of a written section. Academic-minded families around the world raced to tutors to ensure success on the life-defining gatekeeper to college entrance.[4]

That was then; this is now:

- Today, according to Kiplinger, Mandarin and Farsi are the top languages in demand—not Japanese.
- Companies like Google, Apple, and all things tech took KKR's place in the headlines.
- The SAT scoring system changed back to a 1600 scale in 2016.[5]

Because things change. Change itself is the constant. So why place our precious self-worth in the hands of performance or perfection, which live in a perpetual-motion environment?

Thanks, but no thanks.

"I'm not sure you realize how much you're loved," I said while wiping my daughter's tear-stained face as we stood in her tiny bathroom. "Loved by me for sure. But my love is so far from perfect or painless. I'm sure my love comes with all sorts of undertones and messages so many of which I may or may not even be aware." It's true.

44

Whatever was stealing her thoughts that day had a vise grip. My words didn't seem to be getting any farther than my mouth, which really made my heart skip when I looked at her hands and noticed caked blood around the cuticles that she had been nervously pulling—a sure sign that stress was winning.

My heart ached, and I prayed. What else can you do?

"Sweetheart, I wish I could learn this one for you, but I can't. I'm with you, right next to you, and you're going to get to the other side of this. But you don't need the other side to be okay. You're loved, accepted, and okay today. God made you *you*-nique and placed you in the world with a hardwired plan and a purpose for life that will somehow tap into all the ins and outs, the good and bad woven together. And I'll do all I can to help you carry that load until you can do it yourself."

Be Overwhelmed by Purpose Rather than by Performance

Performance pressures are a part of life. Forms are necessary. As are résumés. As are applications and business cards.

Performance pressures become overwhelming when we define ourselves by such things. We define ourselves according to the boxes we have checked (or have not checked)—and inevitably how our checks compare to those of others. And boxes can do a number on us as we try to amass checks and build résumés in the race to perform, because we're all just people, people with sneaky little self-doubts hiding below our well-crafted exteriors. Which is where I found Snopes, smack-dab in the middle of one of life's heightened box-checking phases—college acceptances.

Rather than be overwhelmed by performance pressures, we can instead be overwhelmed by purpose and unique giftedness. But seeing, recognizing, and celebrating such things can be a challenge in our show-me culture. We all have something worthwhile to offer, even if it might not be revealed by a lengthy résumé.

45

You're Gifted

Giftedness is the unique way in which you function. It's the inborn core strengths and natural motivation you instinctively and consistently use to do things that you find satisfying and productive. Your giftedness is not just what you can do but what you were born to do, enjoy doing, and do well.

While other factors such as IQ, personality, environment, and upbringing certainly play a role in shaping your life, giftedness expresses your essential personhood—what makes you, you and sets you apart from everyone else. You're not just a "type" of person. You're one of a kind!

Bill Hendricks,
president of the Giftedness Center
and author of *The Person Called You*

We all come out of the womb with a natural giftedness created to bless those with whom we share life. But we often let thoughts of less-than stifle the use of our gifts. Or we long for a talent or gifting du jour—whatever might be in vogue at the moment.

Some phases of life lead us to question the existence of said giftedness. It's so easy to see it in other people, especially those who tend to be the ones seen. In the midst of day-to-day mundane life, the big picture can get a bit blurry. As a result, we get lost in performance pressures rather than hone the skills unique to who we are.

Because each of us is a person with originality, with giftedness, and with potential. Unique, worthwhile, beneficial, life-enhancing giftedness lies within each and every one of us—as personal and individual as a fingerprint. And with this giftedness, we can tap in to our own unique purpose.

Purpose, at its core, is the common strand that ties gifting together. Purpose is the soul of giftedness, spurring giftedness's use for the good of more than simply ourselves. Purpose grounds. It gives reason. And it taps into that loving-others aspect of life—a reflection of God's kindness.

> Everyone is gifted—but some people never open their packages!
>
> Wolfgang Riebe[6]

For years we got to watch purpose lived out, up close and personal almost every morning—driving from one school to the next. I am often reminded of a certain carpool ride not so long ago.

"Boxster! Hey man! Good to see you! You have a great day. Work hard." All topped off with a loud "Whoot!" by our school's off-duty Dallas Police Department traffic officer, Le'Shai Maston. Then, to be sure his message was heard, Le'Shai pointed in our car window, catching the eye of my shotgun passenger.

Boxster looked out the window with a sheepish grin and nodded. We had just dropped off one kid at our first carpool lane of the morning and were turning out of the school's drive, heading for school number two.

This greeting mirrors the one from the day before. Every day, rain or shine, sleep or an all-nighter, Le'Shai acknowledges the people in each car that comes within a quarter of a mile radius of his location. The result? Hundreds of smiles each day, thousands a month, practically countless over the years.

As we U-turned and made our way past the school, and past Le'Shai, one last time for the morning, I looked at my shotgun passenger as we heard one last *whoot*.

"How does that make you feel when Le'Shai stops and shouts to you that way? When he says your name?"

"Uh, it feels good. Really good."

Whoa—a response! Which means he's listening. I'm running with it. "Remember that," I told him, "what it feels like when someone does something small like smiling and calling you by name."

The great thing about the car is that conversations are shoulder to shoulder with limited eye contact—something I've noticed can

47

be a positive, especially when communicating with teenagers. So there's that and the seatbelt. Nothing like a captive audience.

"In fact," I continued, "look at what Le'Shai is doing to each and every person he comes into contact with. He doesn't even know the people in those cars passing by him, but he points, waves, whoops—making each driver feel like a million bucks. Directing cars might not seem like a big deal, but Le'Shai takes that job to a much deeper level. He takes it down to purpose—what he's doing is making a difference in the lives of each person whose path crosses his."

Le'Shai knows what he's doing. He influences lives every morning in a highly unlikely way—a deeply meaningful way that would never be found as a box to check.

Le'Shai hasn't always worked for the proud blue. Before Dallas PD, he achieved the pinnacle of what every boy thinks would make his life complete: a career in the NFL. A college All-American, he played for Houston, Jacksonville, and the Washington Redskins. But people he regularly sees might not know he played professional football—he never broadcasts his fame. He's not that kind of guy.

I kept on pontificating to my kid. "Are you getting what's important? Not fame. Not an NFL football career. Not signing with Nike or making a million dollars. Not winning a Nobel Prize, not getting a million views or whatever pinnacle someone sets for himself. None of that's bad. But if checking the box is all there is, life becomes about the boxes—not people."

At this point, I grabbed a spatula to ice the cake with a how I see the meaning behind the message, "What Le'Shai is doing certainly involves doing his job well—he's probably the best—but he also genuinely touches people every day. In his unique gifting, as only he could do, he actively cares for the people around him because people matter. This carpool thing is just a small portion of his job. I can only imagine the impact he has on his beat."

After dropping off kids at Le'Shai's carpool lane, we head for school number two. Within minutes, we see the contrast between purpose and performance.

In the mile preceding the second drop-off, we pass three schools and navigate a very long school zone. In the middle of the zone is a different off-duty Dallas PD officer orchestrating traffic—doing the same thing, just not in the same way. He's crabby and rude most mornings. I take the grumpiness as a challenge to get him to smile. Honestly, who knows what he's dealing with in his life. But, he just harrumphs and ignores day after day.

"Okay, kid. How can you help but see the difference?! How do you feel every morning at this point of our drive compared to our drive by Le'Shai?"

"Crummy. That guy's mean."

"Please remember this today, the power of the smile," I beg. "And maybe take the time to actually share one with someone, to say their name when you see them as you go through your day."

Le'Shai, tapping into his vast giftedness, exhibits what's important in life. Hard work. Never quitting. Never letting boxes define you. Being all that you can be right where you are. But most importantly, encouraging others. Which he does every day, whether directing traffic in a carpool lane, coaching kids on a football field, or covering his beat. And I know he has significant stress and pressures in his life—just like I'm guessing the other off-duty officer has. But with Le'Shai, the world's pressures and trappings clearly are not the boss of him—at least they're shelved while he pours on morning encouragement day after day, like a huge cup of made-to-order coffee in a to-go cup.

With examples like Le'Shai, maybe my kiddos will catch on sooner rather than later to what's important in life: people not performance.

Our unique purpose begins to deflate society's pressure-laden burdens to be someone, to be seen, and to be *the best* as it quietly, steadfastly steers us away from performing toward resting in who we were created to be.

But where do we place our identity? Do we believe that every day when we wake up we have to hustle and perform to prove our worth? Or do we believe that our worth and value on this planet have already been decided and therefore we get to embrace purpose—which still involves action—over performing.

We are going to believe something. Why not Truth?

Finding Grace in a More-Is-Better World

Sometimes I feel like we live in the epicenter of performance stress. Our little community nestled in the heart of Dallas could be described as performance pressures on steroids. Which might be true since every community has some driving force that tries to inform our identity. But we also have lots of nice people traveling alongside.

My friend Katie recently tried to ring my doorbell—it doesn't work—while out on a walk one day. I loved that she stopped, realized the doorbell must be broken, and came on in for a cup of coffee and a chat anyway. As we caught up, our conversation moved to our kids, which inevitably led to talking about the stress and the pressures they face. Was it the same for us when we were young?

"Looking back," Katie thought out loud, "I realize my dad just wanted to inspire excellence. But I wasn't measuring up to his expectations. I didn't know what my best was or how to achieve it. He couldn't relate to me so he tried to spur me on, but it just damaged our relationship and made me feel unaccepted." I adore Katie and her honesty. She makes it easy to be real. And I know I had the same issue with best. Pressures to be the best plagued me in my early years as well.

After taking a sip of coffee she added, "We learned so many great things about hard work, never quitting, staying the course—

all things that come with parents who have a drive toward academic performance and success. And I wouldn't trade those things for the world. But the pressure is so much greater on our children now. The competitive nature of year-round sports, social media, college applications, and scholarships make finding a balance really difficult. I watch my kids struggle under what they perceive as a 'be the best' message too. And I wonder, Is there any way to escape it these days, to somehow get a handle on the pressures?"

The struggle to be the best is nothing new to generations that have grown up in an achievement-oriented environment, whether at home or in an academic setting or when staring at a mirror's reflection or on a field where athletic acumen is the ticket out and up. Achievement marks that become more difficult when inevitable blips occur, bad choices are made, mistakes happen.

All of that also adds to the timeless desire—"I want my kids to have it better than I did." As each generation continues to provide the next with more and more opportunities and higher and higher achievement standards, it's hard not to wonder if there is a ceiling to "having it better." Are we supposed to do ever more? And does this well-intentioned, almost groomed ideology inspire greatness, or does it debilitate?

Katie's father owned and managed a few retail establishments across the Southeast. He built a successful business from the ground up, eventually selling it all to a national conglomerate. He also built a family whom he deeply loved and for whom he desired ample opportunities for them to realize their own dreams.

Katie continued, "I heard Cynthia Tobias, who used to be a teacher and was once in law enforcement, say that 'the most important social skill to teach kids is grace.' Sometimes if a kid acts out, like cheating, she said not to assume it's a character flaw. There might be more going on. Can we look beyond the moment to see the person? To see the struggles? And I was convicted that my kids can use a lot more grace from me and a lot less stress. Of course, this idea should probably extend to people beyond my kids."

"I think we might all need grace—probably given to ourselves."

"I wonder," she thought aloud, "if giving grace to ourselves helps us to be able to give grace to others?"

"Hmm . . . maybe . . . probably."

"Toward the end of his life," Katie shared, "Daddy would steal away to a monastery once a year for a week of silence and prayer. And he would write me letters while he was there. It was in one of those letters that I found acceptance." She smiled and nodded as if she were reading it again right there. "He told me he never meant to love me according to what he wanted me to be. He said he wanted me to know that he loved me just the way I am. When he said that, I began to feel safe and free to be who I am. It really had such a profound impact on my life. I think about his words—his gift—as I love my own kids, my husband, and my friends."

Excerpt from Katie's letter

I never have been good at expressing my love, but during my stay here, I've come to realize how special you are to me and how much I do love you. I love you just as you are. I used to think in terms of loving you if you'd change like I wanted you to, but no more of that. You're fine just as you are.

I want you to feel free to do what you want to without having to please me or do what I might want.

You are a wonderful, loving young lady.

I am so proud of you.

Love, Pop
(Katie's Dad)

"Wow. So good." I nodded. "You know, what your dad said sounds an awful lot like the way God loves us— which might sound trite or familiar, but that shouldn't stop us from saying it out loud." God's love falls in the

> The Golden Rule: Love your neighbor—AND, oh by the way, love yourself.
> Amena Brown[7]

category of mysterious and incomprehensible, especially since it stays the same in good and bad times. How can we ever begin to understand it if we don't talk about it?

"Yeah," she said, "Even though we feel some sort of pressure to perform in order to deserve love or to be loved, that's never been God's love. He loves us the way we are. He gave everything in order to be able to love that way. It's just so hard to believe."

We sat for a minute to let it sink in.

"My dad gave me one of the best gifts ever in that letter. He gave me the blessing of his acceptance to just be me! Everyone craves that," she concluded. "Such a great example of love for who we are, not based on expectations or on what we do."

I thought about Katie's letter after she left. I thought about the words as they related to my kids. But I also couldn't help but think about the people who have the hardest time hearing and believing those words—us.

Maybe that's the place we need to start: being kind, gentle, and grace-oriented with ourselves, steering clear of the pressures we place on ourselves. Maybe then we can be overwhelmed by our own unique gifting and purpose rather than bowing under the pressures of performance.

Water Station

SILENT SERVICE

Over the last few years, in a wonderful effort to promote community service, we might have allowed serving to be about others—but about us too. It's hard to keep it 100 percent about others when kids are required to track community service hours or when social media begs for pics of mission-serving locally and around the globe. None of which is bad in and of itself.

But just for kicks, sprinkle all that good with a few silent serving-simply-to-serve efforts.

Start Small without Saying a Word

We all have plenty of silent service opportunities around our home and daily life. I seem to say it all the time: "Just put their dish in the sink and don't announce it!" Or when driving by someone in need: "Buy that person a burger, don't tell a soul, and use your own money." Or, see the need right next to us: clean a sister's room if she's had a bad day.

Widen the Boundaries—Even When It's Hard

I watched a high school-aged child walk out of the door this morning armed with little sacks of homemade cookies to give to her teachers. Between working on assignments the day before, she baked all sorts of goodies. She added an extra for a friend who has alienated herself from others through doses of rude here and there—an action that can either be popular-cool or social suicide at their age. It was hard for the cookie-girl to be nice to someone who's been harsh. But she fought to find compassion.

And, regardless of the outcome, a lightness in being accompanied those cookie sacks. She didn't get to check a box or log service hours or add a volunteer effort to a résumé. But the bounce in her step spoke volumes.

Right Hand Unaware of What the Left Is Doing

Inasmuch as serving helps someone else, it always makes us feel good. Maybe even better when it's done silently. The power of others-centeredness in motion—it works wonders to dial down Life's Overwhelmed—especially when done on the down-low.

Three

Rather Than Be Overwhelmed by Appearance Pressures, Be Overwhelmed by Beauty

I seldom think about my limitations, and they never make me sad. Perhaps there is just a touch of yearning at times; but it is vague, like a breeze among flowers.

Helen Keller

It happened again yesterday, as it does almost every year—the dreaded swimsuit shopping trip. Few things in life can bring on anxiety like swimsuit shopping. According to a recent survey, the great majority of people would rather go to the dentist, do their taxes, or sit in the middle seat of an airplane than go swimsuit shopping.

The vulnerability, the self-assessment, and the inevitable disappointment make the experience a bit overwhelming. It's a hard have-to, and you eventually reach the point where it just can't be put off, yet again, for another day.

Not only had last year's suits limped their way (barely) across the finish line only to be discarded but the girls had also gotten older. Styles had changed. New and fresh called their names.

So with great hope and anticipation of terrific items to be found, my daughters and I headed to one of our favorite stores. A store I knew would have lots of options. Because when shopping for swimsuits, option abundance is a good thing.

We arrived and beelined for the racks, excited and hopeful. And I prayed. Please let them find something. Please let us agree on styles. Please guard their hearts and allow them to see in the mirror the Truth—a lovely person on the other side of that reflection. Please keep us off the path that is almost always traveled when shopping for a swimsuit, the path where we're tempted at every turn to think less of ourselves. Okay, that tempts our thoughts to wish less—as in I wish I had eaten one less piece of Birdie's birthday cake.

The search for the perfect swimsuit started off well. All was good in the world. We whizzed through the racks. We agreed on styles. We even laughed. We were happy at the options that accompanied us to the dressing room. The fact that three women related to each other agreed was in and of itself a minor miracle.

I started to breathe. Maybe this would be okay. Maybe we would walk away unscathed—maybe even uplifted. Was that possible? Could the words *swimsuit shopping* and *happy* live together in the same sentence? One could only hope.

I was just glad it wasn't me trying on swimsuits, standing in front of a full-length mirror, judging, trying to preempt potential judgment by others.

Then it began.

Under what seemed to be the harshest fluorescent lighting ever invented by man, standing in front of a three-way mirror intent on highlighting every flaw, spirits started to tank. And I quietly wished I had taken the girls shopping separately.

As one complained about her poochy stomach (that is *so* not poochy), the other secretly wished hers was as flat as that of the complainer. When one found something that might have been suitable, the other decided she liked the same thing. Feigned "you can get its" followed by "no, yous" were topped with "it's the only one that I halfway looked good ins." Frustration and tension grew. It wasn't pretty.

Swimsuit shopping. Does anyone like it? Is it ever smooth sailing? How can stitched pieces of stretchy material wield such forceful power over our psyches? Even for the naturally skinny few—that stretchy material might tempt thoughts toward pride and possibly judgment of others (e.g. *That lady needs to eat one less piece of her kid's birthday cake*). Either way, there's some shaky ground.

My crew walked into the store fine.

We walked out in need of triage.

Truth: The people who went into the store were the same people who walked out. That mirror, those lights, the swimsuits, all the judgmental thoughts had nothing to do with either of them as human beings.

But somehow Truth can get lost in the mix.

Training our thoughts to recognize what's going on in the moment and to dispel temptations to go negative can help us weather the storms and put Overwhelmed in its place. Before we face the moments that attempt to steal joy, why not pile on Truth? Like putting on sunscreen to block harmful rays, we can cover ourselves with reality checks and metaphorically wear them into environments that are inevitably laced with stress and pressures that can land us in the mud and mire of negative self-worth assessments. We can fill in the blank for whatever messes with our thoughts making us think we have to look a certain way to be okay.

Instead, grab hold of Truth and drink deeply from its well of living water in order to be hydrated before, during, and after

Messaging Exposed

- *The world says a swimsuit conveys a lot about who we are as people.*
  - » Truth says a swimsuit is simply a few pieces of water-resistant cloth sewn together, nothing more.
- *The world says a swimsuit, more than its other clothing friends, reveals how we measure up.*
  - » Truth says articles of clothing have absolutely nothing to do with our worth.
- *The world says everyone is looking, judging who's in and who's out, the fine and the frail.*
  - » Truth says one-upmanship based on outward appearance is a game that has no winners and takes no prisoners. It destroys everyone in its path. So why play?

heightened self-assessment situations such as swimsuit shopping or even something as casual as scrolling through Instagram.

Before we even walked out of the store after shopping, I was on it. How dare some ridiculous dressing room with all its cramped quarters and ruthless lighting mess with my people.

Standing in the checkout line, I stopped my pair and fought for their thoughts.

"No," I began. "I know exactly what happened between the time we walked in this place and now. You experienced a ginormous dose of bad messaging, and I refuse to let it lie to you and tell you that you are less than you are simply because of the way you look."

A little girl in her stroller wide-eyed us while chewing on her pacifier.

"Do you think she cares how she looks?" I asked them, pointing at her, thankful for a perfect diversion. How could anyone look at a cute baby and not smile—especially when she literally cooed when we glanced her way?

"Seriously, 4, 5, 6? Do you think she has a clue about her diaper size? No! And would her mood be altered if she was wearing a Huggies or a Pampers? Do you think she cares about the shape of her eyes? The curl in her hair? Whether her thighs touch in all her adorable chubbiness?" They did in all her adorable chubbiness.

The girls looked at me, trying their best to hang on to the funk that had reached in and grabbed their hearts. "Uh, no again," I answered for them.

I could tell by the smirks on their faces that they were either listening or totally embarrassed. "And do you think that the negative message that somehow duped you into thinking that self-worth is tied to a number on a tag or an image in a mirror has something on you?" I was running out of words, which is unusual for me, but I was just so mad at that horrible mismessaging. So I finished with, "Well, it doesn't!"

So there.

I don't know if they heard me. But at least seeds were planted. And quite frankly, I can never hear that message enough. I'm so tired of the trappings of this world and what they steal from people.

It's important to call out appearance pressures and sprinkle in some Truth. Then maybe realize that the person standing alongside us—thumbing through the rack choices, trying to decide which suit to try on and which would never look good—is likely in the same boat and could use a genuine word of encouragement.

Thank goodness we're not in this one alone!

Exercise Good Judgment

Gathering our things after the shopping trip fiasco, I could almost hear their silent thoughts, so many of which surely raced to pictures of how we're supposed to look compared to a reflection in a mirror. And, that *supposed to* ideal runs along the same tracks as performance standards—it stays in a constant flux of change.

Beauty For Women throughout History[1]

Ancient Egypt	slender, narrow shoulders, high waist, symmetrical face
Ancient Greece	plump, full-bodied, light skin
Han Dynasty	slim waist, large eyes, small feet
Italian Renaissance	ample bosom, rounded stomach, full hips
Victorian England	desirably plump, full-figured, cinched waist
Roaring Twenties	flat chest, downplayed waist, boyish figure
Golden Age of Hollywood	curves, hourglass figure, large breasts
Swinging Sixties	willowy, thin, long slim legs, adolescent physique
Supermodel Era	athletic, svelte but curvy, tall, toned arms
Heroin Chic	chic, waifish, extremely tall, androgynous
Postmodern Beauty	flat stomach, healthy-skinny, large breasts and butt, thigh gap

Note: Changing standards run true for men too.

Societal beauty standards so often determine ideal body types—something that tends to be a brutal measuring stick since much of our body type is predetermined, unique to us like our natural gifting and purpose. In the 1960s long, slim legs were the standard—as if anyone can control the length of their legs. In the Han Dynasty, large eyes and small feet were treasured—the latter of which were often forced by feet-binding, a practice that lasted a millennium.

A small foot in China, no different from a tiny waist in Victorian England, represented the height of female refinement. For families with marriageable daughters, foot size translated into its own form of currency and a means of achieving upward mobility. The most desirable bride possessed a three-inch foot, known as a "golden lotus." It was respectable to have four-inch feet—a silver lotus—but feet five inches or longer were dismissed as iron lotuses. The marriage prospects for such a girl were dim indeed.[2]

61

In today's world, women and men are quick to reach for surgical procedures in order to create a desired appearance. Though less extreme, we do the same with exercise, taking something necessary in life and using it as a sculpting tool in order to achieve a look. But our current postmodern standard seems confusing: flat stomach, healthy-skinny, large breasts, and large bottom. How does that even work?

Recently, I had the unfortunate opportunity to meet face-to-face a not-so-fun diagnosis of shingles. Anyone who has had shingles or who knows someone who has had it knows it's painful—and that it can actually be friendly enough to hang around for a longer haul with residual nerve damage. Which mine decided to do. The bad news: I can't exercise the same way I've done through the years. The good news: nerves can regenerate, and we live in a day and age when there are lots of ways to exercise.

So I started swimming. And the blessing that came with my unexpected changeup has been multidimensional, unexpectedly filled with so much goodness. Much of the blessing comes with the place where I exercise. Suffice it to say that cardiovascular is in their name and rehab is the operative word (as should be elderly) which makes it a far cry from a typical gym.

The lure for me was the saltwater lap pool. The bonus benefit: I'm about twenty years younger than most of the clientele. Yes, even over fifty, I'm the youngster. And I can tell you that the locker room conversations aren't about weight or optimal sizes. They're usually about the best brand of walker, the amount and types of meds recently prescribed, or a good roast recipe.

I get to exercise with people who aren't the least bit concerned with trying to prove themselves, or looking a certain way, or doing anything that involves trying to fit in or buff up. They're happy to be alive, and as sweet Florence (age ninety-two!) told me recently, "I just love to be in the water." She walks the pool, up and down the lanes, in her cool water shoes. "It gets my mind right," she told me. "I come to the pool to get the poisons out of my thoughts. Then I have a better day—always."

Please let me be like Florence when I'm ninety-two! Or better yet, today. She isn't exercising to be a certain size, she's exercising because she's happy to be alive and wants to really live, with her thoughts in order and her body fresh from moving in the water or on a walk. Because a workout makes you feel good.

Snopes has been exercising.

She likes working out at the Y—mostly because she exercises with a friend. Or she hits tennis balls with her dad. Jon loves sports and will happily drop anything to head to the tennis court. Or she late-night sneaks out of the house for a run. Her definition of a run and mine differ.

I grew up in a competitive, athletic home. We competed in swimming from very early ages—for me, it started at seven. Scared of the starter pistol and the lights at evening practice, I moved from the pool to the tennis court. I learned the game and followed our natural progression, entering matches to compete. I started running in seventh grade, partly for conditioning, partly to make my then-slim figure even slimmer. One mile turned into two then three to five. I always felt like more was better and longer equaled good.

I'm not sure I've ever known exercising as something to simply be done and enjoyed. Even going on a run or swim today, I hear words in my head telling me to keep my heart rate up for at least twenty minutes, thirty or more is better.

That's not how Snopes views exercise.

"How was your run?" I ask her. She had left the house quietly around nine that night, and it was ten by now. I was impressed at her stamina to last that long.

"Wonderful," she dreamily replied. "I just love it. The moon was bright. I saw a couple of people on their walks. And I really enjoyed the silence."

"Is that why you go at night? The silence?" I ask. Still amazed at how long she ran and now moved by her intentional interaction with the sounds of silence. *How can she run that long without tunes?* And, I couldn't help but wonder, "Where did you go?"

"Kind of all over." Then she relived her exercise routine. "I like to walk around the block once or twice when I begin. Then I run a block and walk a block. I went over past the Stones' house, and I prayed for them. Then down by the Williamses'—which made me think about how glad I am to have Claire for a friend. Then I saw the cutest old couple walking, holding hands, so I slowed down just to stay behind them and watch. It was so cute to see them walking and talking.

"So, after that," she continued, bright-eyed, "I ran to Caruth Park. I stopped right in the middle of the field—my favorite place—and lay down and looked up at the sky. It was so beautiful. There's something about the expanse of the sky. There are no trees in the middle of the field, so you can see almost from one end to the other. The stars and the moon get my mind off things and remind me that there's so much more going on than whatever caused me stress today. It made me feel great—especially in my soul."

Okay. For her, exercise is church.

I was floored when I heard her "routine" and so thankful she shared. I want my exercise to be like hers. Not filled with have-tos or in-order-tos (like in-order-to fit into a smaller pair of pants) but with gratitude and eyes off myself. Apparently, it can be done. I'm not sure I've ever considered exercising like that.

So here you go, a simple soul-hydration, water station tip: exercise—but not to be a certain size. That certain-size thing plants our eyes on ourselves—not really the best place for thoughts to be anchored.

If appearance thoughts are stealing our joy, why not take a walk around the block, because even a simple walk helps to get oxygen to perspective-starved thoughts.

Snopes not only reminded me of that but offered new perspective to a much broader life-giving aspect of exercise. I'm sure the same can be applied to all the things we associate with outward appearance, including our diet. People say that beauty is skin deep, but maybe we need to look a little farther to understand that beauty has little to do with skin and much more to do with soul. So, in case no one speaks the words to you today and since we rarely encourage ourselves, I'm here to say, "You're beautiful." Your beauty is inside and out.

Why don't we exercise not to be a certain size but to clear our minds and gain perspective so that outward-appearance pressures don't steal the joy from things that can help us breathe.

Today I got a small but forced moment of exercise. Rather than be frustrated with the crazy traffic in Preston Center, I let the parking space in the back of the lot be an opportunity rather than an inconvenience. I got to walk. And I actually enjoyed it. I thought about Snopes's approach and looked up so I could see out—away from the day's stress.

I needed a breath of fresh air. And when I saw someone pull out and open the space directly in front of Chipotle (where I was headed), the walk helped me to be happy for the guy who got it, because you never know what kind of day someone might be having or whether a front-row spot could be just the thing to make it better.

Deeper Than Skin

"What do you want for your birthday?" the woman standing in line ahead of me asked her daughter.

We were waiting at the drugstore. They were picking up and I was dropping off a prescription. It's a neighborhood store that not only fills prescriptions but also carries a lovely selection of gifts and sundries. The Pharmacy is a delightful throwback, a place where new customers still fill out by hand a note card with pertinent information. And the cashiers are likely to know your name.

The daughter, who looked like she was either home from college or close to graduating from high school, responded to her mother's question without missing a beat, "Botox."

Botox? I was sort of surprised. How could this beautiful young lady want Botox for her birthday?

Her mother responded likewise. "Botox?"

"Yes," she replied. "Look"—she scrunched her forehead while smiling—"I don't like the wrinkles when I smile."

It was just the three of us in line, and they certainly weren't hiding their conversation. I thought about her birthday wish and had a hard time imagining asking for Botox. Being a huge baby when it comes to needles, I can't imagine the words *birthday* and *shots* being in the same sentence. (See also: natural childbirths because I can't handle an epidural.)

As the mother looked at her beautiful daughter, I think she was searching for a response. "Botox?" she asked again. She turned around to the shelving next to them and started to say, "Let me show you—" but was cut off by her daughter.

"Oh, I already know about Frownies," the girl said. I had never heard of them, but Frownies are all-natural facial patches for a wrinkle-free appearance, without the need for surgery.[3] "But that's not what I want."

My heart went out to the mom who I knew couldn't help but see the person standing in front of her not as a young adult but as that adorable, without a care in the world, kindergarten-girl she had been several years earlier. "You're too young for Botox," she told her.

The man in front of us completed his transaction, and the pair stepped up to the register, greeting the cashier by name and making kind inquiries about her family. Another register opened, so I took my spot. I handed off my prescription and waited while the clerk checked to see if our medication was available.

At the register next to me, the cashier was trying to talk to the daughter about Botox. "You don't need Botox," she tried to convince her. "You're so young."

"I do." The girl maintained. Then she started flipping through the pictures on her phone, proving the existence of wrinkles when she smiled.

"Well, you're right," her mom agreed. "They're there."

"I think they make you beautiful," the cashier told the young woman. "Not everything about any of us is perfect. That really is the beauty of it."

The cashier had a point. Here comes Perfect again. This time not weighing in on performance but our outward appearance. And again—the thing about Perfect is that it's not real; it changes. (See also: beauty standards through the ages.) But her point can be hard to believe in the face of the world's standards. And our relationship with those standards can stick with us for a long time, opining on our self-worth. For whatever reason, we sell ourselves short, especially in the category of outward appearance.

Dove, in one of its inspiration-via-advertising campaigns, presented women in Delhi, London, San Francisco, São Paulo, and Shanghai with a challenge. At the entrance to a shopping center in each city, the company placed signage above adjacent doors. Upon entering the building, women could choose to go through a door labeled "Average" or another labeled "Beautiful." Dove filmed the results, offering a compelling commentary on how women tend to view themselves.

I don't think it's a surprise that most chose the "Average" door.

In an effort to encourage women, "Dove interviewed 6,400 women between the ages of 18 and 64 in 20 countries around the world about how they perceive beauty in themselves and other women. Ninety-six percent of the women surveyed said they don't see themselves as beautiful, but 80 percent believed every woman has something beautiful about her."[4]

With those statistics, why not err on the side of finding things we like about ourselves rather than spending so much time thinking about the things we're lacking or would like to change? We think it of each other—why not ourselves? Rather than be overwhelmed by where we fall short, why not be overwhelmed by all we have—the good things? Maybe we need to reach yet again to gratitude.

Bobby Rodriguez, a friend and youth minister who has spent years as a CrossFit instructor and deeply cares about fitness, calls a healthy perspective *surrendered wellness*. "There's such a fine line between fitness and health," he shared with us during an interview on the video podcast I cohost, *SaySomething Show*. Bobby goes a step farther and describes stewardship associated with both.

"Where we have to change as a society," Bobby told us, "is innovating a path of understanding that the standard we are all trying to achieve is not how we look in relation to everyone else but how we steward our bodies. My son in elementary school tended to be chunky—not overweight—but he thought something was wrong with him because he would look in the mirror and struggle with not looking like everyone else.

"Stewardship," Bobby continued, "allows our relationship with our bodies to not be about a size, a number on a scale, and all those things we can manufacture to measure self-worth. Instead, we can land on the fact that God gave us a body to live out a life on earth. Then we can go to, 'How can we steward our bodies to have the highest amount of energy, feel the best, communicate the best, think the clearest?'

"If we're looking to surrender our wellness, the work that we do to steward our bodies well (exercise, eating right, consistency) produces ancillary benefits that are often those we desire. But rather than be stuck on the treadmill of what we did, we have freedom—which allows us to enjoy those benefits more."[6]

Maybe it's at that point, free from so many of society's elusive beauty markers, that we can be content, even, dare we say, be grateful with our size, gray hair, and wrinkles. Honestly, I see my gray hair and am grateful. Grateful for the rides on Central Expressway in five o'clock traffic with new drivers behind the wheel. (I could literally feel the hairs turning gray—eek!) Grateful for the years that have passed—even the hard ones that likely sprouted a few more gray hairs than I could have imagined possible. Those years not only provided provision perspective for today but they also filled my compassion tank to overflowing. I can commiserate with hurts I might have been tempted to judge if I couldn't empathasize. I understand challenges and sadness. I know what it's like to watch someone you love hurt, year after year. Those hairs are a physical representation of age but also a physical manifestation of stress. Even though I feel very little stress in my soul since I know without a shadow of a doubt that all is well, we cannot avoid living days of pressures, stress, and hard circumstances. The fact that they really aren't the boss of us undeniably girds those days and years with deep, unshakable peace in the midst. And I'm grateful to those hairs for the reminder.

And I'm grateful for the wrinkles, some from worry, so many more from laughter that accompanied us on long roads. Reminders that light reigns not only on the other side but in the midst.

Because just as the sweet pharmacy cashier encouraged the young girl, *"Not everything about any of us is perfect. That really is the beauty of it."* Why not be overwhelmed by that?

Water Station

SPEAK IDENTITY-TRUTH OUT LOUD

A seventh grader at Queen Creek Middle School in Arizona offered her classmates a reminder about what's important in life through a poem she wrote for an assignment. The assignment was to write a poem on a topic about which the student was passionate. Olivia Vella, on the front lines of all things middle school—not the least of which centers on body changes and appearance pressures—based her poem on a common plight: "Why am I not good enough?" Her powerful message was captured on video. And, once reported on by the local CBS affiliate (KPNX-TV), it garnered over nine million Facebook views in two days.

In her poem, Olivia methodically chronicled a day in the life of a young teenager struggling with insecurity and a desire to be popular. The day begins and ends with a mirror—an identity message board of sorts.

"As you gaze into the bathroom mirror, you see a stranger that somehow stole your reflection and replaced it with a completely different girl. You tell yourself, 'I just want people to like me. I just want to be accepted.'" [7]

Then Olivia noted all the day's struggles to fit in, to be okay, to be accepted, accented by the gross mismessaging perpetuated throughout society's definition of such things.

The poem outs the elephants in almost every room. "Society infers girls have to have skinny waists, tan skin, long silky hair, perfectly straight teeth. . . . Society infers girls have to wear tons of makeup to look pretty. Society infers girls have to wear skanky clothing and do inappropriate things with boys to be happy and considered cool." [8]

We are so quick to, almost blindly, buy into societal messaging. But we don't have to. Why not just as quickly give Truth a chance?

Why not hear it and believe it rather than be overwhelmed by ever-shifting yet oh so powerful cultural standards?

Teenage Olivia herself, wise beyond her years, takes us there. "Society is wrong," she said. Then she begs us to reframe the message and instead be overwhelmed by the Truth: "You are loved. You are precious. You are beautiful."[9]

four

Rather Than Be Overwhelmed by Image Pressures, Be Overwhelmed by Image Bearing

> So God created mankind in his own image, in the image of God he created them.
>
> Genesis 1:27

My family's life is about as far from a beautifully crafted, social media highlight reel as you can get. It's more of a highlight *real*.

Take this morning, for example.

I hit the snooze on my alarm at least five times. My great intentions of getting up early for a few quiet moments to myself failed. No worries, though. The snooze button and I are close friends. We interact almost every day, multiple times before the sun rises.

I finally got up, woke up Fury who needed to study for a test, and headed downstairs. As I reached to light the fire (an absolute must on

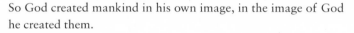

72

a chilly morning), I saw a roach. And by roach, we're talking a Texas water bug, as in cockroach on steroids with wings. I don't know why, but they often try to find their way inside after a big rain. I put on my brave face, grabbed a shoe, and attempted to hit the disgusting thing. Of course I missed, and it somehow disappeared. All I could do was hope that it went under the house—or somewhere far, far away.

So I moved on. Fury sleep-stupored his way downstairs and grabbed his books. Then he settled in next to the fire—until something ran behind his back. Screeching, the kid jumped up and yelled, "A roach!" as it scurried under his binder.

Needless to say, I wasn't going to let that thing escape another time. So Fury and I teamed up to kill the intruder. He bravely lifted his binder, and I smacked and smacked and smacked (once more for good measure) the bug with the kid's shoe.

V-I-C-T-O-R-Y.

As soon as his sisters came down, he told the tale of how we had been victorious. Then came finger-pointing at the one who had left crumbs when eating by the fire—a clear rule violation. That kept going, as did the victory story, all while I was trying to cook a breakfast that required little chewing, since two of the kids had gotten their braces tightened the day before.

For once, not only had I actually remembered the orthodontist appointment but we had also gone. No need to mention that I might have gotten the kids out of school the day before and shown up for the appointment a day early when the doctor was at their other office. How exciting—we got to go to the ortho twice!

After I finished making breakfast, the kids grabbed their scrambled eggs, moaning each time something passed their lips, touching sensitive teeth. The eating stopped the minute we heard a frantic scream from the living room. Birdie, freaking out, ran to me for safety after throwing his shoe across the room. Apparently, dead roach had a sibling who had nestled into Birdie's shoe that had been by the fireplace overnight.

It was freaky. Seriously, who wouldn't be unnerved by feeling a roach in their shoe? We were all a little shaken.

But again, trying to be brave, I went to the couch where Birdie had been sitting when he had discovered the creature. The bug had fallen out of his shoe and was on my couch! And I was like, "What? Seriously? *Two* in one day!" We hadn't seen nary a bug in our house for almost a year, except for the fake ones that Snopes puts in my path to cause heart stoppage.

Again, I took a deep breath and bravely Dudley-Do-Righted in to save the day by killing the beast—or not.

Yes, I missed again.

Not only did I miss but I also somehow managed to push the bug *into* the couch. Where it remained, and still remains, as far as I know. Because we never found it. How would we ever sit on our couch again? If I were that roach, I'd stay amid the springy, cozy darkness and wait. I'm guessing he knew with absolute certainty that in a home with this many people, some wayward kid would once again forget the food-in-the-kitchen-only rule and leave a few crumbs in a cushion.

We survived breakfast and headed to the car for school, slightly dazed by the morning's events.

A dead bird was just outside my car door. I would be finding the shovel when I got home to dispose of that lovely item. Then en route to school, Fury remembered a book he needed, so we circled back and he mad-dashed in and out of the house because minutes matter. It's a school-tardy domino effect for us.

Birdie, still reeling from his roach-shoe experience, was slumped in the backseat, grumbling. He had decided that the morning's trauma absolutely warranted a free day home from school. His mean mom disagreed.

We dropped off one kid and raced to the next school.

"You know, you're not supposed to drink and drive," Birdie mumbled at me from the backseat.

"What?" I asked.

"Yes. I just watched you drink. And you're driving."

"Honey, this is coffee," I said, holding up my green mug from Kohl's, the Christmas present from the kids that I had gotten for them to give me. "No drinking and driving means a beer or something like that."

"It doesn't matter. Since you did that, I should get to stay home from school."

Okeydoke. At least he was tenacious, and creative, and attentive to the rules. If only he would follow the food-in-the-kitchen-only rule.

We got to school. Fury hopped out. Birdie took his time.

"Birdie, get out, honey. We're holding up the line," I encouraged.

He slow-motioned his way out the door, monotonely grumbling, "I love you, Mom. I hope you have a good day. I won't."

As he got out, a stray piece of trash flew after him. Now not only had we held up the line by a slow-motion exit but a wrapper was also yet again flying about. My little rule follower raced after the trash, his backpack flopping around, and grabbed it. He headed back to our car, opened the door, and put the stray wrapper back in.

The carpool monitor smiled at me, as did others as I drove past after having held up the line while my child was bounding after flying trash.

A good start to a regular day. Regular, scary, hilarious, embarrassing—still peppered with "I love you, Mom" in the midst.

By the time we got to dinner, there was nothing to eat because we had never made it to the grocery store. So we did what we sometimes do: drive-through. This particular time, takeout went extreme, catering to every taste. We hit Chick-fil-A, Wendy's, and Chipotle in one fell swoop. Except Chipotle doesn't do drive-through.

So we split the pickup. Snopes drove through the lines while I ran in to get a burrito bowl for her brother. All was well until I stepped up to pay and saw an empty wallet. Whatever cash I had found in my wallet had been handed to the driver. And, sadly, there wasn't a credit card to be found.

There I stood holding up another line, wondering what to do.

"You come here all the time," said super-nice Chipotle cashier guy. "This one's on me."

"Seriously?" I could barely believe it.

"Absolutely!" he smiled.

I snapped a pic, posted it on Instagram, shared the short version, captioning it with "Love that!"

It's real.

It's life.

It's a far cry from so many of the pressures we feel to present a curated image of a perfect life. I'm sure such pressures have always existed. Norman Rockwell, print commercialism, television, and all sorts of messaging tools have communicated the way of the day. But since the technology explosion, it can be hard to get a break from the reach and incessant nature of society's image pressures.

Strange how those image pressures so quickly and easily win out over reality and all things regular. But the intensity just might be the fuel we need to be able to say no to the pressures since allowing these things to inform self-worth significantly affects our ability to tap into the truth of our identity.

The tired conversation that we can't stop having about social media's curated nature of perfection means we deal with image issues and anxiety a lot of the time. But rather than strive to create the perfect image and rather than let another's seemingly perfect image have something to say about us, why not opt instead to see behind the "seens" where there's always more than meets the eye?

And it's usually a load of regular.

Pictures fade but people stay. People who—like everyone else—simply long to belong, to be known, and to be loved. People whose significance far exceeds any labels or identifiers that drive image creation.

Identifiers

Identifiers play a major role in our self-worth. They include things such as professions, sports teams, colleges, families, groups, and even gangs.

Identifiers tend to find life based on what we value. In broad terms, Washington, DC, thrives on power; in New York, money drives; in the Northeast, education and intellect; in the Northwest, a different kind of green—the environment. For kids today, it's fame.

Over the last several years, there has been a significant shift in aspirations for young people. Years ago, when asked the question "What would you like to be when you grow up?" kids tended to respond with an occupation: teacher, doctor, fireman, etc. But ask a kid today, and he or she is likely to be a bit more vague. According to a 2014 survey, the top two answers given to this question were rich and famous. When asked whether they thought money could buy happiness, three-quarters . . . of the youngsters said yes.[1]

Peter Tait, former headmaster of Sherborne Preparatory School in the UK, urges us to pause and consider the implications. "Such responses may be dismissed as symptomatic of the times we live in and society's obsession with fame and money, but the implicit lack of purpose and ambition to 'do' rather than to 'be' prevalent among our children should concern us all."[2]

The issue is found on both sides of the pond and in other parts of the world. "With the rise of reality TV and social media, everybody can be a celebrity and fame has currency," said Lauren Greenfield, author of *Generation Wealth*, a photo collection documenting societal trends of the last twenty-five years—especially those having to do with image projection of financial well-being.

She explained, "The thing about this project is: It's not about the rich, it's really about our aspiration to wealth, and our needing to show it off whether we have it or not."[3]

Her conclusion after over two decades of gathering pictures was this: "We've never had more inequality and we've never had less social mobility. So, in a way, fictitious social mobility—bling and presentation—has replaced real social mobility . . . because it's all you can get."[4]

Greenfield believes there's been a shift in values, from "hard work, and thrift, and frugality and modesty" to "bling and showing off and narcissism."[5]

Identifiers are now based on and driven by image creation. Curated pictures posted on platforms tell the story. Then they do what we can't seem to stop them from doing: inform us about ourselves in relation to others as well as to our own expectations.

Kate Fagan talks about the power of identifiers in her book *What Made Maddy Run*. Fagan, an ESPN writer, covered the heartbreaking story of Maddy Holleran, a freshman NCAA athlete at the University of Pennsylvania who died in part at the hands of image creation.

Maddy struggled under the weight of identifiers. A highly decorated student athlete, she didn't know what to do when she joined other high school superstars at the NCAA level and "best" became "top quarter." She started to get lost—to no longer be the person (according to her identifier as top athlete) she knew herself to be. Stress set in, as did disappointment in herself and the weight of disappointment she thought others must be feeling about her as the result of her letting them down. Social media's life-is-perfect pictures from all those around her added to the mix and prompted Maddy to take an action that could not be reversed.

Her story reveals that when we face difficulties, human nature leads us to think we are the only ones feeling a certain way. Nothing could be farther from the truth. Honestly, any issue that lands us in an I'm-the-only-one camp is actually a flashing red warning sign that we're walking into an inaccurate self-assessment minefield.

If we're healthy, with our self-esteem anchored in Truth's solid ground, we can manage identifier pressures. As with all issues that feel overwhelming, we can try to find balance while enjoying the process—all of the process, whether arriving at or coming short of landing hoped-for goals—without allowing the product to take too much ground and overinform core confidence and self-worth.

What if identity and image management pressures can be toned down as we consider the deep significance, though rather interesting concept, of image bearing that goes back to gifting and purpose rather than image creation.

Identity over Identifiers

A stack of coins perfectly sorted and positioned on the credenza in our living room provided proof that our Future Hoarder of America had been dipping his toes into his favorite pastime. When Birdie was little, he hoarded almost anything. Random items looked like treasure to him: game pieces, acorns, bars of soap, sticks of butter (yuck), and countless other things that he would stash away for safekeeping in his bed, under cushions, and sometimes in our home's central vac. I thought he had grown out of it—but maybe not.

I guess he finds comfort in finding, organizing, and stashing—an activity that has taken a break over the last few years. Hoarding is a fairly benign coping strategy—if that's what it is for Birdie. Or he could simply be bored. But I've noticed an increase in quiet periods when he goes through drawers—most of which are chock-full of junk—finding things and secretly gathering. Again, since B, I find myself more aware of actions that resemble coping behaviors and want to stay ahead of it.

"Are you okay?" I asked him, noticing his pockets bulging with loose change.

"Can I have a baggie?" he asked, nonchalantly putting his hands in his pockets as if nothing was going on.

"For the coins?" I outed him. He can't stop the blush that reveals he feels busted. "It's okay," I assured him. "There are baggies in the drawer that you can get. But is everything all right?"

"Umm . . . yes?"

"Come back after you get your baggie. Let's look at what you've found."

Identity plays such a big role in reframing Life's Overwhelmed. What a challenge it is at all stages of life to believe that our identity can be anchored in more than labels or identifiers. Due to my life stage and that of the people with whom I travel life, I find myself in an almost daily battle with a kid's grade identifiers. Just this morning I noticed someone's fingernails practically nonexistent, since they had been nervously picked to the quick. For this child, grades are fighting to gain ground. "Sure, grades affect you," I implored. "But they just don't inform who you are as a person."

Barton rolled her eyes, audibly sighed, and shook her head. Identifiers are loud and tend to drown out reason. But I get it. They're all around us at every life stage.

I was a tiny bit under the weather recently. I rarely get sick. And getting sick as a mom—well, it's not like the BK (Before Kids) days when you could exit life and snuggle into bed with a remote control close by and ample opportunity for silence as desired. Any bed snuggling or quiet these days has gone the way of the dinosaur. Just stealing away is a feat in and of itself.

But I tried, despite multiple interruptions in the form of drink requests, referee appeals, and homework questions. Then the kids, at least the few who still fit into the young category, couldn't stop themselves from sitting by Mom on the bed. And with my cover blown, all the kids, and sometimes their friends, kept trickling in. Then they would change the station from whatever sappy movie in which I had found momentary relief to Nicktoons noise.

Did they not know how bad I felt? Probably not. Because, to them, I'm Mom.

But during one moment alone, I watched a little *Notting Hill*. William Thacker (Hugh Grant), an owner of a travel bookstore, and Anna Scott (Julia Roberts), a mega movie star, make an unlikely pair until she explains at the end of the film that apart from fame, "I'm just a girl, standing in front of a boy, asking him to love her."[6] Cue the tears. So sweet. Run after her, Hugh. She's just a girl. Regular underneath it all.

Dialogue preceding the declaration actually sets the stage with what we tend to believe defines us. Listen in to William's reasoning as to why a relationship with Anna just won't work.

William: I live in Notting Hill; you live in Beverly Hills. Everyone in the world knows who you are; my mother has trouble remembering my name.

Anna: Fine. Fine. Good—good decision.

Pause

Anna: The fame thing isn't really real—you know. And don't forget—I'm just a girl, standing in front of a boy, asking him to love her.[7]

Out of the two characters, the one identified with life's coveted fame and fortune label is actually the one in the equation who clearly understands the fleeting and irrelevant nature of labels. They're momentary. They change.

Yet we can't help but define ourselves and others according to them.

Recently, someone who was new to Dallas referred to me as "HP girl" in a text. I slightly cringed.

HP signifies the area of Dallas in which we live. And I couldn't help but wonder, *What does she mean by that? Is that what she thinks about me? Is HP good? An indictment?*

I struggled with being identified and not knowing the meaning behind the designation—it could be so many things. And I wasn't sure I liked the options. I wanted to text back, "I'm not HP girl. I'm just Kay." But I found myself at a loss. If I said something, doing so would shine a spotlight on the label, and I wasn't sure she meant anything at all by it. It was probably my own issue, not hers. And she's so nice, likely meaning nothing by it. I fought my ping-pong thoughts and chalked the label up to a part of life—though I was surprised at the slightly overwhelming feelings of insecurity that flooded my thoughts, probably due to being at the mercy of a label from someone I barely knew instead of just being me.

I don't think I'm alone. My college-age daughter had just been sharing with me how she doesn't like telling people where she's from. "I just don't like someone assuming or even concluding something about me—good or bad—based on where I live." We all do it. When I lived in DC, just telling someone I was a Texan conjured up all sorts of assumptions. I'd probably proudly agree with most of them—except for having a cow or an oil well in our backyard or at one point knowing J. R. Ewing.

And with people, labels might classify but they don't define even if we think they do. A person is more than a label.

Yet human nature tends to compartmentalize and place. We make designations and then arrange them as if we're in a grocery store. We shelve the classifications of ourselves and others so we can easily locate and retrieve items when needed. The Corn Flakes go in the breakfast aisle. Chicken nuggets go in the frozen food section. Healthy items can be found in fresh produce: organic, good; locally grown, even better. Snacky man-made items are scattered in the center aisles. Once labeled, we are placed and assume our distinctions.

But a person isn't like a box of cereal whose contents both enter and leave that box as cereal. People are fluid, moving in and out of and so much more than labels. A high school all-district, celebrated quarterback may or may not be able to take that label to college, causing some serious questioning when expectations inevitably offer their very loud opinion. Which is where Maddy Holleran found herself. Not only in a place where the labels had started to mismatch reality but also in an environment lived out loud online.

> The life Madison projected on her own Instagram feed was filled with shots that seemed to confirm everyone's expectations: Of course she was loving her first year of college. Of course she enjoyed running. Her mom remembers looking at a photo on her feed and saying, "Madison, you look like you're so happy at this party."
>
> "Mom," Madison said. "It's just a picture."
>
> Everyone presents an edited version of life on social media. People share moments that reflect an ideal life, an ideal self. Hundreds of years ago, we sent letters by horseback, containing only what we wanted the recipient to read. Fifty years ago, we spoke via the telephone, sharing only the details that constructed the self we wanted reflected.
>
> With Instagram, one thing has changed: the amount we consume of one another's edited lives. Young women growing up on Instagram are spending a significant chunk of each day absorbing others' filtered images while they walk through their own realities, unfiltered.
>
> Kate Fagan[8]

From the outside looking in—though some identifier labels actually last forever, US presidents are always presidents—people are more than a label. They're people!

From the inside looking out, it's up to us to control label perception rather than allow it to control us. We need to fight to make labels descriptors rather than definers.

83

From a faith standpoint, again, it's not who we are but whose we are. We are individuals, with value and dignity, created with unique purpose. Made to be image bearers rather than image creators.

Birdie returned with several baggies and dumped his stash on the table where we began to sort. I thought the coins offered a perfect reminder.

"You know, each of these coins is really just a blank piece of metal," I tell him. "It's the image stamp that determines the coin's identity. A quarter and a dime look exactly the same—a sheet of metal—before they are cut into different sizes and sent through a machine where an image of George Washington or Franklin D. Roosevelt is literally pressed into the metal. After that the coin bears the image of the die. The metal doesn't do anything but receive the stamp. A dime isn't willing itself to be a quarter. And a quarter doesn't have the ability to become a penny. Its identity is what it's intended to be." Sometimes I get going and don't stop. It's just that there are so many reminders around us every day that point to identity over identifiers.

"And it's not just coins," I continue telling Birdie. "Things like plants and trees are the same. Like Barton's basil." I pointed out the window to a gathering of herb pots. Our resident chef decided she wanted to grow her own herbs—not from a starter plant but from seeds. She'd been watering and caring for them daily. And I'd be the first to admit that her killer tomato sauce does taste better with her freshly cut basil.

"That basil is not willing itself to be basil or wishing it were parsley. It's growing based on what it is. Like an apple tree bears fruit—apples, not oranges or lemons."

Then I turned to Barton, as she stressed over grades. "Sweetheart, the identifiers like grades or varsity or what-

> What you do, I cannot do. What I do, you cannot do. But, together we can do something beautiful for God.
> Mother Teresa[9]

ever tempt you to think they make you who you are. But they don't define your identity as a human being. All anyone can do is their best and lean into being who they were created to be, not what the culture of today says they should be."

"I know, Mom," she replied. "It's just hard when the pressures are intense."

She's right. And she does know. I've watched her step in and fight for her friends as they battle their own thoughts.

Culture's do-all/be-all life often seems to make more sense than living as an image bearer. Probably because *bearer* isn't a word we hear very often. Bearer sounds weird, heavy.

C. S. Lewis shed some light in his famous sermon "The Weight of Glory"—there's more to our story than simple existence. If we can understand the more-to-the-story, maybe we can take hold of the mystery of whose image we bear.

> There are no ordinary people. You have never talked to a mere mortal. Nations, cultures, arts, civilization—these are mortal, and their life is to ours as the life of a gnat. But it is immortals whom we joke with, work with, marry, snub, and exploit—immortal horrors or everlasting splendours. . . . Next to the Blessed Sacrament itself, your neighbor is the holist object presented to your senses.[10]

It's hard to grasp the great worth—the inherent worth—of a person.

The I'm-just-a-girl admission plea sits perched on all our tongues, begging to be spoken and heard—probably mostly heard by ourselves. Because despite the many hats we wear—keeping every plate spinning, smiling, encouraging, staying one step ahead—we are people. Regardless of identifiers and labels, we're all people needing to be loved and reminded that we each have purpose and worth.

Perhaps we need to remember to treat and be gentle with ourselves the same way we are directed to treat others. Is it possible to

Beyond Labels

In October 2015, headlines around the globe read something along the lines of, "Harvard's Prestigious Debate Team Loses to New York Prison Inmates."

An inmate label, especially with a maximum-security descriptor, inevitably brings with it certain connotations—none of which land at Ivy League or debate or victory. But with a dash of belief and a load of preparation at nearby Bard College, inmates at Eastern Correctional Facility in New York, a maximum-security prison, defeated the Harvard debate team that just the year before had won the national championship.

"The purpose of work is not to reform criminal justice per se," Max Kenner, founder and executive director of the Bard Initiative, said, "but to engage and to relate to people who are in prison, who have great capacity and who have that dedication and willingness to work hard, as we engage any other college students."

The debate proved that there's more than meets the eye, especially when people are involved. Rather than label, Kenner saw the person who, though in prison, had the capacity, dedication, and willingness to work hard, just like the people called students at Bard College.

And sometimes people need help to see beyond their own labels. "'We have been graced with opportunity,' Polanco, who [was] in prison for manslaughter, told the *Wall Street Journal* after the debate. 'They make us believe in ourselves.'"[11]

Perspective and a couple of reminders can go a long way toward protecting ourselves from label overreach.

consider the famed theologian's words with a clear motive and a sobering perspective—to linger and contemplate, to consider what is beyond that which can be seen with human eyes.

I don't know. I move from deep ponderings back to the moment.

"Does any of it make sense?" I asked Barton, getting back to the conversation at hand.

And then Birdie decided to jump in. "I'm just trying to save money to go to the Lego store."

For goodness' sake. No coping going on here, just gathering.

"You know this isn't your money." I looked at him shaking my head as he continued to organize and stash the mass of coins.

He shot back the cutest smile. "Well, I did work hard finding it. Isn't there something for me in that?"

All that coin gathering for Legos, not stress relief.

I guess it wasn't something deeper. It's hard not to be on constant alert these days. Still, maybe Barton and I both needed a reminder today—a little whose-we-are not who-we-are hydration to fill our tanks before we hit the hills. Maybe leaning into Truth, whether we grasp it all or not, helps us learn and understand and trust. To be overwhelmed by the freedom in image bearing, in being who we're created to be rather than get bogged down by almost endless image pressures.

Torn Seats and All

"There's a side to you I never knew, Kay Wyma," my friend Brooke said as she smiled. We were last to leave the morning gathering. "Yes," she continued, "I learned a few things about you last week—from your car."

New things about me from my car? My mind raced to grab hold of anything tangible that might give me a clue.

Then I remembered.

Oh my goodness. My car!

She had been so very nice the week before to run to my car to grab something for me. I had been on deck to lead our Tuesday Bible study on heaven. Introductions of the morning had been made, the makeshift recording had started, when I realized I didn't have my book. I saw Brooke and whispered, "Hey, could you run to my car and grab my book?"

Johnny-on-the-spot, she jumped right up and turned for the door. Then she asked, "What do you drive?"

"The dented white Sequoia parked on the far right." Yes, still dented from the time a nice young man had crashed into us a few years earlier.

She slipped me my book upon returning, and off our group journeyed on the very interesting, challenging, hope-filled road of considering the topic du jour—life in light of eternity.

So as I stood in front of Brooke and my mind raced to put together the "I've learned a few things about you" pieces, it didn't take me long.

She'd seen the inside of my car and duly noted its appearance. Though our car's outside has issues of its own, the inside—now that's raw. I mean, it was summer. Kids, kids, and more kids had been in and out of that thing.

The weathered (some might say torn) seats, the wrappers, the Slurpee cup that may or may not have sat in a cup holder for a week, the swim towels, the extra shoes—one waterproof pair, which came in handy at Costco the other day when a storm blew in and I didn't want to ruin my new sandals—the list really could go on. The inside of my car—like the inside of our closets, refrigerators, drawers, etc.—had added a new dimension to her knowledge of me.

I guess she learned that I'm not lying when I say I haven't got it all together. She got to see up close and personal our very regular life. We're just a family of seven that comes with a lot of stuff. We come to the show regular—with lots of love and few expectations of perfection, sprinkled with a dash of procrastination for good measure.

Yes, my car said much to my dear friend Brooke. "The torn seats?" I asked her.

"Yeah," she sweetly replied. "And a little more."

Brooke's nodding smile warmed my soul. And all the wonderful aspects of authentic friendship—even friendship that is relatively new

> You have to keep unmasking the world about you for what it is: manipulative, controlling, power-hungry, and, in the long run, destructive. The world tells you many lies about who you are, and you simply have to be realistic enough to remind yourself of this. Every time you feel hurt, offended, or rejected, you have to dare to say to yourself: "These feelings, strong as they may be, are not telling me the truth about myself. The truth, even though I cannot feel it right now, is that I am the chosen child of God, precious in God's eyes, called the Beloved from all eternity and held safe in an everlasting embrace."
>
> Henri Nouwen[12]

(we've only really known each other a couple of years)—washed over me. And I melted into vulnerability and acceptance. She was meeting me in the midst—not running away or gasping or whispering.

She wasn't judging me.

And so I refused to judge myself. I held tight to the thoughts that tempted me to freak out. You know the ones. *She saw our mess! What must she think of me? Everyone else has their stuff together. What's wrong with us?*

"I love you even more," she announced.

I think the key for most women is not only ditching the judgment of others but also slowing down the often misguided, overly harsh labeling and judgment of themselves.

Why don't we determine to train our kids and ourselves to self-access in the light of how God sees us? To focus our attention on striving for excellence as it relates to our best—not *the* best. To let God's light rather than culture inform what we see in the mirror. To consider perspective rather than latch on to a glimpse.

Instead of giving in to image pressures, why not remember that we're actually created, as human beings, to be image bearers. Rather than give an inch to tempting thoughts that drift toward places of comparison where we might think that someone else's life looks better than our own, let's gravitate toward gratitude for all we have and were created with unique purpose and gifting to be. Why not see the whole scene including the "seens"? Because almost every image has the good, the bad, the ugly, and lots of regular just below the surface. In the same way, the people in the picture also have spectacular gifts woven deep within, making them who they are rather than who they need to be.

SEE IT—SAY IT

Even though there's no easy fix, reframing and reminding ourselves of Truth can go a long way. How do we make that happen? The solution involves talking.

See It

When we wake up with heaviness or start to feel overwhelmed during the day, recognize it for what it is and call it out.

I recently had coffee with a friend whose marital situation had taken an unexpected turn. She has lived some hard days of unmet expectations and loads of heart-hurt both for herself and her daughter since her husband left. Finding solid ground has been a challenge over the last couple of years, especially for a mom who so desperately longs to shield her kid.

Even though I'm not traveling the same road, I understand. We all have life-twists that can leave us weak and wondering—territory that should never be entered alone.

While I grabbed our order, she glanced through her phone.

By the time I got to the table with our steaming hot, heart-foam-laden lattes, she looked a bit down, feeling overwhelmed.

Say It

Thankfully, she felt safe and was able to be honest.

"I just saw a pic, and I have to say my heart aches." She couldn't stop herself from allowing a picture of smiling happy couples to inform her situation. "It's ridiculous, I know, but I look at them and want to be them. And am reminded that I'm not."

Rather than let the threatening thoughts take root, we talked aloud about Truth—that is equally at hand—opting instead to be overwhelmed by life-giving perspective.

"You know that's just a picture," I reminded her. We *all* know that pics are simply a moment, far from reality, that include a backstory for everyone. A little reminding goes a long way. "It's a moment, not the whole story. Remember my family's Christmas card?"

She nodded.

"Yeah, well there was a lot more going on in the background of that genuinely terrific photo—including lots of crabbiness, a few tears, and even some boys who decided to sneak off into the storm drains. It's amazing we even got a picture."

Overwhelmed begins to be reframed by Truth. Truth that the people in those pictures matter, that they're just people who feel the same way we all do. Truth that what is going on in someone else's life isn't informing or defining ours. Truth that we are seen, known, and loved by the those who walk alongside us. Truth that solid footing can be found even on shaky ground.

In the most beautiful way, my friend takes it home—beyond the picture to hope.

"I've read," she said, "that God takes ashes and makes them beautiful. And, I guess I'm getting to see it happen even in our seemingly horrible circumstances."

She went on to tell me about her daughter and around twelve of her friends who have a safe group text where they have committed to be honest and discreet. "They even have a safe word—a regular word that means, 'Something is going on. I don't want to talk, but I need to. Someone call me.' So my daughter did and does. It's amazing watching her help people."

In the midst of hardship, mismet expectations that are unfair and even unthinkable can absolutely overwhelm—especially when our kids are involved. Dare we look beyond to see more? I loved that my friend was fighting to do just that.

"I mean a group of teenage girls' refusal to play the game or to be victims to things like people talking behind their backs or hurting each other's feelings or even *much* bigger issues has been proof to me that love is alive even in great disappointment."

See It—recognize that something heavy is weighing in and threatening to steal the moment.

Say It—call out Life's Overwhelmed and start to reframe it by countering the world's messaging with Truth.

Why give stress and pressure-laden overwhelmed more ground than it deserves when we can be overwhelmed by Truth with all its grace and hope and peace and love. The things that actually are the boss of us.

Just breathe.

five

Rather Than Be Overwhelmed by Formulaic Right-Way Pressures, Be Overwhelmed by Perfect Imperfection

> Look beneath the surface; let not the several quality of a thing nor its worth escape thee.
>
> Marcus Aurelius

"I probably said too much, but what was I supposed to do?" I wondered aloud while munching on an amazing salad at the Nasher Sculpture Garden. "Live in a vacuum? I can't imagine that being healthy."

"What's going on?" the friend I was eating lunch with asked.

"One of our kids is struggling. I'm sure most of it is just life, but it's shredding my heart. I'm hurting, and wondering, and worrying, and trying, then messing up, then apologizing. I think I've been trying to figure out if we're okay. Figuring out aloud."

"So what's wrong with that?"

"Well, I was talking to a friend on the phone, and she decided to help by pointing out things I could do differently and giving me answers." I paused, then admitted, "It felt like she was dishing a load of judgment. Basically, she told me I was coming up short, which actually hurt more than helped. Then in all my suppressed-teen emotion, I sassed back at her, 'Why don't you come live my life and parent these kids yourself? I'm sure you can do a much better job than I can! I guess I'm not perfect!' Then I changed the subject and did my best to get off the phone. I was pathetic."

My silence begged her to fill it. She shrugged her shoulders and added, "Sounds like you're the perfect mom for your kids." She smiled matter-of-factly and continued, "Sounds like you're living life, doing some great stuff, making mistakes, then apologizing. Which means you're the perfect mom for your kids." She took a sip of her drink, then added, "Sounds good to me."

I wasn't sure if I bought it, but she sure was nice.[1]

The underlying pressure to get life right, as if there is a right way, can be so wearisome. It's like we've put a rubric in place to inform our progress. Rubrics, "a guide listing specific criteria for grading or scoring academic papers, projects, activities, and tests,"[2] are everywhere—not only in our kids' classrooms but also in countless other areas of life.

In theory, a rubric offers guidelines—guidelines that are good and helpful and necessary. But in practice, rubrics can promote the letter of the law rather than the intent. And in doing so, they sometimes serve as a gateway to doing things the "right way," which can also make them a deterrent to exploration, to experimenting, to creativity, and to learning. And whether we like it or not, a significant portion of learning occurs during the prone-to-make-mistakes, outside-of-the-box, phase of the process.

Rubrics, though helpful, can add fuel to culture's trend toward performance. We so desperately long for there to be a right way for everything—quantifiable rules to follow so that results are guaranteed. But life just doesn't work that way, especially with people at the center.

I watched every bit of air being sucked out of my kid's sails the other day after he got an English paper back. And I couldn't help but think, *what a shame.* The rubric convinced him of something that is not true. He felt stupid, even though he isn't. And yet thanks to the rubric, he can prove to me that I'm (the one telling him: *you're a good writer, you can work on the grammar and spelling, creativity counts for something*) wrong.

Though education-related rubrics are tangible, many of life's rubrics aren't. Magazines at the grocery store checkout reveal the latest standards for fitness or organizing or status, and Pinterest and Food Network might lead me to believe that my kitchen and menu need to reach a certain standard in order to invite people over for dinner:

Dinner Party Evaluation	Overall Score: Sufficient—75%
Kitchen	Very Good—100% Recent remodel, stainless steel appliances, large open space conducive to conversation, guests felt welcome
Dinnerware	Unsatisfactory—5% Paper plates and folded paper towels for napkins—fail
Food	Sufficient—55% Slightly charred pork tenderloin and bottled versus homemade salad dressing offset by the from-scratch cream puffs dessert
Conversation	Satisfactory—80% Fun conversation starter questions under each guest's placemat. Next time don't include "most embarrassing moment"

It's such a fine line. Can rubrics and hands-on, creative, failure-laden learning coexist? I think they can. At least I sure hope so. But I think marrying the two takes a lot of time, patience, and trust. Something I hope we can remember along with the boxes that beg to be checked, because in our home tender hearts need room to navigate life inside *and* outside of them.

After lunch, I raced to my car, which had been sitting in an unseasonably hot December sun. Opening the car door, I noticed a strange but familiar smell. One that didn't quite fit with my car. I tried unsuccessfully to place it. It wasn't foul. Just out of place.

Late for carpool as usual, I ignored the smell, grateful it wasn't something worse, and zipped north onto the tollway. Around Mockingbird Lane, I placed it. The smell wafting from my back-seat was Windex. Then I remembered my Target run a few days earlier. One of the kids had called while I was out to tell me we were out of cleaner. So I had bought two jumbo bottles and put them on the floor behind my seat. Within minutes of my leaving Target, the same kid called back to say she had found the Windex and not to worry.

Life had gone on, and as is often the case in my less-than-perfect world, I had forgotten about the backseat bag of Windex for a few days. Until I smelled it.

Hidden under some school papers, one of the bottles had broken open. Not only was my floorboard soaked but so was my youngest child's school sweater.

I raced home and dumped the soaked items on the front porch— why hide it?—and threw the sweater in the wash before returning to carpool duty.

As riders piled into my car and commented on the smell, I shrugged it off as a fresh, clean result of our now uncluttered car.

That Windex seems to be the story of my life. A call for help. My attempt to solve the problem. The "never mind." Inevitable distraction by other issues. The resulting mess. My attempt to clean it up. Everyone keepin' on.

Things rarely go as planned.

Never perfect.

Then I thought about my friend's perfect-parent comment. And I decided she was right. Life isn't about being perfect. It's about doing our best and leaning into "perfect imperfection."

As I hugged my little guy good-bye the next day, I tried to hide a smirk as I caught a whiff of his cologne. The Eau de Windex, despite a washing, was a sweet reminder to me that my kids don't expect me to be perfect. They do expect me to stick with them. To stay by their side. To encourage them on the hills and loops of their inevitable roller-coaster rides. And to breathe easy with them as they coast on the straightaways and gear up for what perfect imperfection lies ahead.[3]

Imperfect Embraces Differences

If there were only one right way in life, how could differences—which we all have and which the world needs—exist? We are all different. We entered the world different from everyone else, fingerprints to prove it.

I get to see different up close and personal every day, since the people with whom I share life are each completely different, even though they share the same last name. They came out that way. Even though I ate and acted and exercised during pregnancy pretty much the same way with each child (okay, so maybe exercise got less and less with each child—by number five, it felt like my insides were falling out if I walked around the block), the kids were different from the get-go.

And the differences come out all the time. It's easiest to see them when the same task hits each of their plates. Take, for instance, the driver's license.

I'll never forget sweet Snopes.

"So when I get in the car, do I look at him?" The test was over a month away, but she was already—and had been for months—mentally preparing for it. Because that's her MO—she thinks about things *a lot*!

When I took my driver's test, I don't remember thinking about anything except parallel parking. I tried to get it right countless times, but I struggled to master missing the curb. Maybe it had something to do with the little attention I paid to my driver's ed instructor, who on the day of parallel parking literally came to the tennis center where I was playing in a tournament and picked me up. It's easy to recall the colossal embarrassment as my name was announced over the loudspeaker, not to direct me to a court but to call me out to the parking lot, where my teacher waited in the school's beater Chevy topped by the ginormous "Student Driver" sign he had hoisted and locked onto the roof.

It was so bad.

My instructor, determined to finish up the last lesson and to cross me off his list, had gotten my parents' blessing to head my way and get the hours done. Remember—small town, West Texas. I was the last student needing to complete driving hours that kept being bumped by something "more important." I think he was done with my excuses, as were my folks.

So there I was, in the tennis center lot, practicing parallel parking with everyone watching. How could they not? There might as well have been a strobe light attached to that "Student Driver" sign. Prayers of thanksgiving were raised from all areas of the tennis center: "Thank you, Lord, it's her and not me." So I can't imagine why I struggled with that section of my driver's test. I still cringe thinking about practicing in that lot.

Thankfully, when the day of my driving test came, my older brother told me I could totally botch the parking and still pass as long as I didn't hit the cones. That's all I needed to know.

But not Snopes.

"If I look at him, the driver's test man—because I'm pretty sure it will be a him—do I say hello or ask him how he's doing, you know, if he's having a nice day?"

I could almost see her palms sweating.

"Because," she continued, "I would do that in real life. You know, ask someone how they are. That's what I do . . . but I don't

99

know if you can talk to the man while taking a driving test—or if he will think I'm asking him because I'm trying to be nice so he will pass me."

"I don't know," I told her. "Maybe ask him if it's okay to talk to him."

"Okay, yeah, that's good. I'll ask."

Then she started thinking about what to do or not to do. "Sunglasses or no sunglasses? You know, can I wear them? Radio or no radio? For sure no phone. Do I adjust the seat or not? And visor or no visor?"

My goodness.

"My friend Paige told me that putting the visor down blocks your view. So she didn't put it down, and she didn't wear her sunglasses, so she could barely see a thing. But she just kept going. She didn't know what to do when the sun blasted in and she was afraid to touch her visor."

For Pete's sake!

"Listen, the idea is to be safe," I assured her, trying to add some perspective. I think she was quickly losing sight of the purpose behind a driver's license test. "I'm pretty sure he'll be okay with sunglasses or visors. Just ask. He's a person. Like you. He had to take a driver's license test once too."

"Oh . . . yes . . . okay . . . yeah, that's true." She nervously laughed, trying to reassure herself.

I raised an eyebrow and wondered what else was going on in that mind.

It's what she does. She mentally considers every detail of every road she meets or might meet. *Every* detail. What should, would, and could happen has already been dissected by the time something happens. It's actually kind of sweet. It's who she is. Still, I can't imagine the amount of mind power spent on all the variables.

Yet I'm convinced that her little exercise is part of what makes her, her. She has an uncanny sense of her surroundings. And because of that, she sees things most people don't. She's been that way since she was a little girl. And most of the things she notices are people who often go unnoticed but desperately need to be noticed. Still, with heightened awareness comes some oversensitivity—perfectly imperfect.

She's different from her siblings. Her sister Barton, the super-organized and matter-of-fact, *whatever* girl was the one to get in the car and go, wearing sunglasses and putting down the visor. She has, and has had since the beginning of her life, an *I-got-this* approach. She was my child who took a stance even in the labor and delivery room. After twelve hours of hard labor, I'll never forget the nurse offering an epidural—something that I had sworn off because I thought the baby was about to be born. That thought, along with my needle phobia, had me saying, "This baby is for sure a boy—stubborn and stuck, determined to do it his way. What a surprise to see a girl. Her matter-of-fact way can sometimes come off bossy, but that determinedness and no-nonsense attitude is what has allowed her to step in and on many occasions to stop Life's Overwhelmed from bullying people—perfect imperfection.

Then there's Fury whose perfect imperfections come in the form of passion and tenacity that each morph into anger some-times. I've watched them used for good on many occasions and hope he will always use them that way—maybe to find the cure for cancer.

Those are just a few of the people in our house. Different can be hard. Different can be challenging, especially when right-way pressures voice their opinions and judgment around every corner.

I guess that's where faith and good friends come in. Faith that calms rough waters. Faith that offers assurance that God has gifted each child with purpose and has placed them with the right parents who can love them like no one else. Faith that, with our hearts and intentions in check—not acting out of fear or in people-pleasing mode—everything will be okay. And friends who, with loving discernment, can help us see a bit more clearly as we manage differences.

Is there a right way? Why do we so desperately want there to be one? *Can* different be okay?

Often the judgment that comes with the right way is harsh. One of my children came to me recently because her best friend had overheard another mother offering negative commentary on the way my daughter had chosen to do something. The situation crushed her and caused her to wonder if the choice she had made—a choice that wouldn't have instant results but a decision made wisely—was right.

Frustrated that this mother was talking to others rather than to us, I tried to refocus my daughter's attention. "Sweetheart, if you had made the decision in some sort of manipulative way or to avoid or control an outcome, then we would be having a different conversation. But you didn't do that. So don't worry. You acted wisely, sought advice, weighed the options, and acted. When making big decisions, people often try to confirm they've made the right ones by comparing them to the decisions of others. And if their decisions are different, we sometimes justify ours by putting others down."

I know she's seen that. People do it all the time. We tend to feel better when the crowd is with us. Differences can make us feel unsettled. And when we are faced with differences, we can sometimes do things we normally wouldn't do—like put someone else down in order to make ourselves feel better.

"Honey," I continued, "I don't think she meant anything bad. Even if she did, assume the best, and do not let overheard remarks steal your peace."

I watch different, maybe best said "unique," play out in front of me every day. Unique people are right next to me as well as traveling alongside. I've always admired people who are comfortable in their own skin—maybe the key is having our hearts in the right place. With hearts in the right place, we do our best to steer them toward the good aspects of their uniqueness and away from the bad.

So sunglasses or no sunglasses? More often than not, I think it doesn't matter.

Imperfect Embraces Failure

Watching Birdie rummage through his backpack to pull out the day's homework, I noticed a growing pile of homework corrections in need of attention.

"Sweetheart, what's up with the stack of uncorrected corrections?" I had to ask. But I didn't want to ask. The avoidance was looking more purposeful than regular forgetfulness.

"I hate school," he replied.

Okay, he really doesn't hate school. He actually enjoys it and loves learning. Not all kids love to learn but Birdie is a curious soul. He's intrigued by the way things work, interested in history, and almost always asking questions that dive deeper than the surface—like "what's the meaning of life?" On top of all that, he adores his teacher.

"Honey, hate is a strong word, and I'm pretty sure you don't."

"Oh, I do," he insisted.

Clearly stuck in traffic on that road, I looked for a way to inch forward on another. "What's up with your homework? It's like you'd rather not do it than make a mistake."

Silence.

"Are you afraid of messing up?"

Silence. Big eyes began to moisten.

I love that boy's eyes. They tell it all. There was likely more attached to the situation than simply answering a homework question wrong.

It is a challenge living in a world obsessed with the idea of right-way perfection.

Albert Einstein would struggle now even more than he struggled within the cultural standards of his day. Thank goodness he didn't cater to the right way of his day. Lee Smolin of *Discover* shared:

> Physicists I've met who knew Einstein told me they found his thinking slow compared with the stars of the day. While he was competent enough with the basic mathematical tools of physics, many other physicists surrounding him in Berlin and Princeton were better at it. So what accounted for his genius? In retrospect, I believe what allowed Einstein to achieve so much was primarily a moral quality. He simply cared far more than most of his colleagues that the laws of physics should explain everything in nature coherently and consistently. As a result, he was acutely sensitive to flaws and contradictions in the logical structure of physical theories.[4]

How interesting that Einstein was moved more by a moral quality than by life's pressures or societal norms—even when those norms were related to the science community of his day. I wonder if we're brave enough to anchor ourselves to moral standards rather than to societal norms.

Einstein's ability to see flaws and his fierce refusal to compromise had real repercussions. At the beginning of his journey, his professors did not support him in his search for an academic job, and he was unemployed until he found work as a patent inspector in Bern, Switzerland. He could have stopped there and settled for what the world had to say about his ability to contribute to the whole. But he didn't.

As human beings, with a soul and a purpose, we must not settle or hand the reins to societal norms. But to rest in and cultivate purpose can be a challenge when living in a day and age that celebrates instant, that wants today's answers yesterday, that equates slow with inadequate rather than taking needed time to reach for excellence on the other side of deep contemplation. It can be hard to opt for moral quality and to be uncompromising in the pursuit of Truth.

Famous Failures

Thomas Edison was told by teachers that he was too stupid to learn anything. He was fired from his first two jobs for not being productive enough. Even as an inventor, Edison made one thousand unsuccessful attempts at inventing the light bulb.

Nobel Prize–winning, twice-elected prime minister of the United Kingdom **Winston Churchill** struggled in school and failed the sixth grade. After school, he faced many years of political failures, as he was defeated in every election for public office until he finally became the prime minister at the ripe old age of sixty-two.

Henry Ford failed in his early businesses, which left him broke five times before he founded the successful Ford Motor Company.

Harrison Ford was told by movie executives that he simply didn't have what it takes to be a star.

Vincent van Gogh sold only one painting during his lifetime, and this was to a friend and for a very small amount of money. While van Gogh was never a success during his life, he plugged on with painting, sometimes starving to complete his over eight hundred known works. Today they are worth hundreds of millions of dollars.

Michael Jordan was cut from his high school basketball team. Luckily, Jordan didn't let this setback stop him from playing the game. "I have missed more than nine thousand shots in my career," he said in a 1997 Nike ad. "I have lost almost three hundred games. On twenty-six occasions I have been entrusted to take the game winning shot, and I missed. I have failed over and over and over again in my life. And that is why I succeed."[5]

We, like Einstein, live in the world the way it is—though much faster and quicker to judge than it was over one hundred years ago. So how can we promote purpose and giftedness and learning in an environment obsessed with performance? I'm not sure, but one thing we've discovered along our way off the perfection road is to talk out underlying issues and internal conversations.

"Honey, learning is filled with lots of mistakes. In fact, it's hard to learn—genuinely learn—without messing up."

Birdie was listening, so I kept going. "Teachers know that mistakes come with their territory. They even welcome them. Mistakes help teachers know what we do and don't understand. They help them to be better teachers and us to be better students. Don't be afraid of making mistakes."

It's true. I think we forget the major success stories that are literally peppered with mistakes and failures.

Then I offered, "The reason your teacher wants you to correct your work is because she cares about you."

Dubious, he looked up. I knew he was listening. I prayed he would hear. "She wants you to learn. She doesn't want you to look the other way, pretend you know something when you don't, or worst of all, quit. The truth is it would be a lot easier for her to mark something wrong and move on. But she cares for you more than that."

As I came to the end of my little life lecture, I hoped I would hear what I was telling him since I, too, am faced with challenges and making mistakes every day. "Please see those corrections for what they are—a statement that your teacher, a person willing to air your mistakes, is actually for you and wants you to be all that you can be. See those corrections as a little note of encouragement, not a sign of disappointment or a statement that you are less than others. No, they're a sign that you're worth the effort."

Talking. Perspective. They almost instantly helped him. Sometimes a little story behind the story—a view of the way things are rather than the way we perceive them to be—can go a long way.

Imperfect Is Perfect with Our Audience of One

Whenever asked, I go with Barton as she walks a neighbor's dog. She jumps at any opportunity to care for a pet, which she would do for free. But she gets paid for this job. And for me, I jump at almost any chance I get to walk with a kid, even though she speed walks and can't help but remind me, yet again, how old I am as I huff to keep up.

"Come on, old lady," she quipped as she switched between a little jog, a speed walk, and a pause for Nike, the Havapoo rescue wonder dog. He looked at me with the same get-with-it glance back. I guess he thought I was slow too.

But I used to be athletic. Yes. I was fast on the tennis court. I wasn't fast in cross-country or track, but I wasn't slow. And I could run a long way. My kids don't realize that I even took them along on my runs when they were little. I'd pile them all in my eye-catching, triple-baby jogger, put our dog Sadie on her leash, and off we'd go. My neighbor Dom would hilariously predict future pregnancies based on when I was "back in shape," because as if on cue, the minute I was back up to the mileage I liked, a plus sign would appear on a pregnancy test and running would take a forced hiatus.

So maybe I have slowed down a bit. My runs aren't as long. And they might have a hint of leisurely associated with them, if and when they occur. But rather than calling myself old and decrepit, I prefer to frame my slowdown as time purposed for enjoying and lingering rather than racing through.

Yeah, Barton doesn't buy it either. But on a pause during that day's speed race, we passed the cutest garden tucked alongside a side-yard fence. It had a few flowers, some dormant shrubs, and a sign that spoke into the day. It simply read:

Between these weeds
My flowers grow

"That's kind of like life," I said as we both stopped to consider the words while Nike sniffed the ground.

"That's why I like to plant a garden," she reminded me, "from seeds."

"Why not a starter plant?" I asked.

"Oh, I don't want a starter plant. I like watering the seeds and watching them sprout and grow—or not grow. They may or may not make it like a starter plant, but I feel like I know better how to do things when I mess them up."

This kid is not afraid of failing. The other day she wanted to cook something "I've never made before." Upon deciding to try popovers, inspired by one of our all-time favorite programs, *The Great British Bake Off*, she warned, "But just know they're going to taste terrible. I almost always mess up on the first one or two or three." She laughed. "But I learn how to do something well by making mistakes and figuring out what works best."

I have a lot of extra pounds to attest to the making of those mistakes and multiple attempts at baking. Maybe that's why I'm slow. But she's not afraid of the mistakes, and some amazing successes have not only grown up in the midst of those weeds but have also overtaken the garden.

Slowing down to see and to read and to consider that sign offered just the perspective we needed in order to reframe Overwhelmed. The truth in that sign speaks volumes into today's overwhelming pull toward right-way perfection—a ruthless measuring mark that steals from the person from whom it begs pursuit.

I like Donald Miller's saying: "When you stop expecting people to be perfect, you can like them for who they are."[6] Which I think we can quickly agree with—until we make ourselves the subject of that admonition. As in "When you stop expecting [yourself] to be perfect, you can like [yourself] for who [you] are." I'm not sure why it's so hard. Maybe we need the greatest reminder of all, the one that can completely reframe persona pressures that draw so much life from a right-way obsessed society, we're performing for an audience of One. Hmm . . .

Water Station

EXPECTATION PRESSURES

Expectation mismatch is a phenomenon that every person from every walk of life across all the ages of time has dealt with. But rather than be overwhelmed by them, why not reach for some Truth?

We're Not Alone

Dana Perino, former White House Press Secretary, author, and television personality outed her own struggles: "At 25 . . . I was racked with anxiety, filled with fear, and totally confused about what I was going to do with my life. I felt like everything I'd visualized for my early adulthood wasn't coming true, even though I had an enviable career path, good friends, no debt, and a supportive church group."

Expectations Are Ideas Not Reality

I'm reminded of Beatrice Prior, the heroine in Victoria Roth's book *Divergent*. In a dream-induced state Beatrice finds herself literally fighting for her life in a glass box that is filling with water with no way out. As she searches to find an escape, rising water fills every crevice. She begins to give into the fear of suffocation until she remembers—"It's not real." It's a dream state, not reality. She gently taps her finger on the inch-thick glass box. The glass shatters.

Tap the Glass with Perspective

The world's pressures, like expectations, are like the water rising in that glass box. They overwhelm and try to control the conversation. They ebb and flow, shifting with the winds of the day. Today it's a job title. Tomorrow it could be a home, or marriage, or kids. Yesterday it was a homecoming date or a college acceptance letter. But these things are momentary.

Perspective taps and shatters the glass. Yesterday's expectations don't carry the weight today that they did in the moment. Just like today's expectation pressures will seem insignificant when tomorrow's stress captivates our thoughts.

So rather than taking that bait, force a look around to see the bigger picture and breathe. Consider all the unique, God-given, individually endowed giftedness in ourselves and those around us.

Remind Ourselves of True Value

A friend of mine signs her email, "Humbly yours," followed by her name. She follows her signature with this quote: "A humble person is one whose status compared to others [or *to expectations*] doesn't matter to him because his value in God's eyes is a settled issue."[7]

Six

Rather Than Be Overwhelmed by Group Pressures, Be Overwhelmed by Belonging

> The greatest difficulty is that men do not think enough of themselves, do not consider what it is they are sacrificing when they follow a herd.
>
> Ralph Waldo Emerson

"If I'm not on the soccer team, I won't have any place to sit at lunch," Fury said to me in a sort of nonchalant way. He may have been floating the announcement to test its validity.

He was on the cusp of a major life change: moving from middle school to high school, from forty-five kids in a grade to five hundred in a grade, from everybody-knows-your-name to we'll-try-to-know-your-name-by-Christmas. He's a gritty kid who can make his way, but the daunting unknown had him testing the ground to find something solid.

"What are you talking about?" I asked. We were driving, as usual. "Who told you that you have to be on a team to have a place to sit?"

There are some conversations in life that I encounter and never want to have again. This was one of them. I can barely stand societal messaging that identity and self-worth are somehow attached to a group.

"It's true," he continued. "I have to be on a team in order to have a place at lunch."

His statement took me back to when I too heard those words when the kids were tiny. But they were attached to a certain preschool. In our neighborhood, moms of itty-bitties would rouse themselves from the minuscule amount of slumber they might have gotten in order to stand in line at three in the morning to secure a coveted spot in the program for their baby or toddler so that—and yes, these were the words—*they would have a place to sit at lunch at the elementary school.* Elementary school? These kids were barely crawling. How could a Mother's Day Out program have a voice in future years far from that sign-up date. Apparently, getting in that preschool would be a make-or-break moment. Which, news flash, it wasn't.

Group pressures happen at each life stage. And for some reason, a place to sit has a loud voice on whether or not a person is okay.

A-place-to-sit stress has been around for a long time. It doesn't take much for memories to flood my mind. They take me back to the hall leading up to my junior high school cafeteria—that room in which we ate lunch, laughed with friends, collectively cringed at a tray crash (thanking God it wasn't us), and dug through the trash can on more than one occasion to find a lost retainer. It was also the place I most dreaded my first week as a seventh grader.

En route to the pressure-laden location, I walked with my friend June, unsure. Seeing the cafeteria doors with all the intimidating social aspects just on the other side, I couldn't help but feel stressed.

Questions crowded my thoughts. *What if we can't find a spot? What if everyone already has a place? Should we be walking in with three or four people instead of two? Should I be with someone else? Is June cool enough? Am I cool enough for June? Who should we sit with? What if there's only one seat?*

I guess the questions took over all available space in my brain, because as we started to cross the cafeteria threshold and scanned for a place to sit, somehow I didn't see the stopper deftly placed on the floor to keep the cafeteria doors from smacking into each other. Not only did I miss seeing it but I also completely tripped over it and landed flat on my face in front of the eighth-grade boys' table. Literally, face-plant, sprawled arms and legs.

As if that weren't bad enough, the table of cute, football-jerseyed boys stood and clapped.

It was terrible.

Sweet June helped me up. Honestly, if I had been her, I'm not sure that I wouldn't have kept walking and pretended not to know me. I awkwardly waved an I'm okay as I limped my way to the food line, where I prayed to be invisible.

We've all been there. Maybe not flat on our faces. But there's something about a seat at the table that makes us feel okay—that signifies belonging.

All that to say, I understood. I heard what my son was saying.

"Did someone tell you that you have to be on the soccer team to have a place to sit?" I asked Fury, wanting to get an idea of the source. If he had come up with the plan, that was one thing. If a group of kids or a parent was trying to establish the rules of belonging, that was another.

He hesitated, then blurted, "Well, football would be the best group, but soccer is probably next best. And I like soccer, so I'm going with that one."

"Okay," I replied. "It's great to play soccer because you like it. But as far as the cafeteria goes, I promise you there are places to sit." Then I started to pray, *Please let there be a place to sit!* And I wondered if he would be as brave as his sister who has been known to scan the lunchroom, see, and then join a kid who was all alone.

Group pressures are real, and they reach far beyond the cafeteria. The world tells us that we need to be in a group to be okay.

It's interesting the way we strive to be grouped. First, we struggle to pick the right one—where to volunteer, which club (workout, social), carpool, or team to join, anything really. Once grouped, we settle in, grateful to belong. But we still cling for dear life lest we find ourselves groupless again. Or we wonder and toy with buyer's remorse: Is this the right group? Is there a better group?

Groups fight to define us. They act as another identifier—answering, or maybe feeding, our internal need to belong.

Belonging

In 1943, Abraham Maslow, an American psychologist, created a pyramid outlining a hierarchy of needs. According to his theory, five interdependent levels of basic human needs (motivators) must be satisfied in a strict sequence, starting with the lowest level, in order for a person to function in life. Physiological needs—food, water, breathing, and the like—form the base. Security comes next, followed by social needs.[1] This is where we find our core needs for love and belonging. They are a part of what makes us human.

In recent years, a new form of human interaction has affected our internal need to belong. Social media platforms involve groups—some that require an invitation, some that are public—inclusion, exclusion, numbers of friends or followers, likes, comments, and more that can't help but inform our level of belonging.

And we use social media platforms often. According to the Pew Research Center, more than 92 percent of teens go online daily, including 24 percent who say they go online almost constantly and 56 percent who say they do so several times a day.[2]

But adults are also affected. Adults on Facebook are especially avid users: 75 percent log on daily, including 51 percent who do so several times a day.[3]

Since social media relies on relationships, in the form of friends and followers, it can't help but feel personal. This is good, but it can bring with it bad. (See also Facebook Depression and Instagram Envy.)

"I'm not on social media or Facebook or anything," a friend recently told me when we bumped into each other at the grocery store. "So it's hard to relate to Sam [her teenager] as she processes and struggles with feeling left out or less than."

"Oh," I sighed. "I get it."

She told me how Sam had come home from camp—a week away from technology—and almost instantly had started to struggle under the weight of her friends' photo feeds. One feed showed her friends' selfie action at the pool. The hardest part for Sam was that one of the friends had only hours before declined getting together with her—something about being forced to stay home and read. *Not.*

"It's not like when we were kids," my friend continued. "Sure, everyone has been left out. I certainly wasn't included on every occasion. But when we were young, being left out wasn't so in your face." She's right. In those days the worst thing was a note being passed through instead of to you. "My heart went out to Sam," my friend sighed. "She couldn't stop feeling left out and unwanted—alone, like she didn't belong."

"It's brutal," I replied.

She lightly smiled and shook her head. "I can honestly say I don't mind being social media illiterate, but I'm thinking I need to jump in so I can help my daughter swim."

My heart went out to my friend.

I get it. I think we all do. Social media, though terrific in many respects, can be ruthless, sometimes taking our thoughts captive in not very positive ways.

It's hard to stay grounded in truth when faced with group pressures or while interacting on internet platforms. But the way we see friends can make a huge difference in our contentment and our sense of belonging. It seems counterintuitive, but the more we see others and contend for the belongingness of others, the more we feel known. If we remember that I'm-just-a-girl people are involved, we can lock away those reflex reactions to negatively assess ourselves and possibly see those walking next to us. Help others know, remind them that they are seen, walking alongside rather than against.

I've noticed that no matter what parental controls we put on our kids' phones, we can't stay ahead of the curve. Things change too fast. We can't go before every cafeteria-type scenario. But we can teach them and help each other learn how to travel roads paved with group pressures.

When a daughter sees pictures she's not in, she needs to remember that real people are involved. When a son sees the lunch-table group, he needs to remember they are real people. When they are faced with group pressures, may they always be aware of the people. May they always remember that each person in the photo, each person in the group feels the same way—worried about being included, fighting to be known, wondering about next time, dying to belong . . .

What if we remember that everyone is just like us? People have the same cares, the same worries, and the same need for acceptance. Why not be overwhelmed by belonging rather than worrying about being left out—especially when we can take note of the fact that more people are at other tables than are seated with any one group. Things we might see if we're looking up.

I caught sight of something on the back of Snopes's phone yesterday—a reminder, maybe a lifeline of sorts—that she had artsy-lettered on paper and popped on the back of her phone case:

I wonder how many people I've looked at all my life and never seen.

John Steinbeck[4]

Her reminder to herself inspired me—and apparently her sister, who saw it and asked for a copy for her phone.

Together Truth

"When I was your age . . ." We've all heard it. I think we all say it. Those words usually involve some reference to hardship.

I used that phrase on a recent drive to visit my brother at the lake. My comment went a little something like this: "When I was your age, my brothers and sister and I endured long car trips every summer. And the air-conditioning was a bit lacking in the backseat of our blue station wagon. We would fight for a spot right next to the tiny vents in hopes that just a few wisps of coolness would come our way."

I think my comment was spurred by someone saying they were hot, which warranted a *let-me-tell-you-about-hot* soliloquy. Or it could have been the motel we passed that reminded me of one of the car-trip vacations my family took when I was a kid. I remember staying at this scary motel. Each of its ten rooms had a tiny little window unit air conditioner and a metal door that faced the smoldering parking lot. Still, that dinky parking lot did have a pool. Which reminded me of how excited we would get to stay at a motel with a parking-lot pool—especially since it had a slide.

"Yes, we didn't stay at swanky resorts when we were your age. And we didn't have phones or iPads to entertain us on our summer trips. No. We looked out the window. Or read comic books. Until we were carsick."

By this time I was sure everyone had tuned me out, but I kept going. "Or we made up games. We mostly bothered each other. And listened to music—whatever my mom chose to play on the 8-track tape player." I had now reached the point of going Dark Ages. "I think I know every John Denver and Barry Manilow song."

I started to sing, "Don't give up on us bay-beh," then I caught myself. "Well, that's David Soul; he was Hutch—I wonder what's happened to him." What was I doing? Thank goodness they weren't listening! I'm sure Jon was thankful for the peace and quiet as he drove in a separate car. Although, he'd probably have tuned out my rambling—or fallen asleep.

I suddenly had an idea, so I snapped the kids to attention. "Hey! I think you guys are missing out. At least look out the window."

At that point, I took everything away and made them look out the window. Seriously, there is a lot of entertaining stuff along Texas highways.

Cue the crickets. We actually passed a tractor—driving on the highway—going 20 mph.

At least they will have a story of how they were all miserable together. Stories can remind us that we belong, that people are next to us, experiencing life with us—regular life on highways filled with tractors that take their time getting to the next exit.

We have ways all day every day to connect on more levels than those driven by technology. Thanks to Boxster, board games have reentered our lives. This kid is a gamer, but not all games involve screens. And even though technology is great, real life is better.

Always.

This summer in our home I've been watching the beauty of human interaction play out—live and in person. And I didn't do a thing to promote it. Boxster did. I think in part because screen systems only go so far.

I'm embarrassed to admit that recently when asked by this son to play a game, I had to force myself to do it. I didn't want to. I had stuff I needed to do. But, thankfully, I quickly berated myself and reminded myself that when the kids were little, I would stop everything for a mind-numbing game of Go Fish. What was I thinking saying no? Seriously, whose young adult kid asks their mother to play a game with them?

So I said yes and pulled up a seat to our dining room table before he changed his mind. We played a new board game that he had recently purchased called Hive.

We talked. And laughed. And he was so kind to me, quietly saying things like "Are you sure you want to go there?" and "You can take that move back and try again." Boy have the tables turned.

We weren't focused on winning. The game offered human connection.

That's the great thing about board games or puzzles, even cooking or, dare we admit it, folding the laundry together. Conversation occurs. Laughter floats. People connect. Sure, they can bring with them the good, the bad, and the ugly of family dynamics. But people keep coming back for more, because these things promote relationship.

So rather than be discouraged by group pressures and the life they find in technology, let's tame them a bit. If we're stuck on a keyboard or our kids can't dial down the demand for likes/shares/retweets, may we gently redirect attention elsewhere and introduce live, human interaction that's engaging and real rather than a dreaded act of endurance.

Technology isn't going anywhere. And the platforms aren't the problem. The groups aren't the problem either. It's fine to be a part of a group. But to rely on or anchor our self-worth in a group in order to be okay proves dangerous. Allowing a group to solidify life's ground can't help but be a dicey prospect. Such ground shifts with almost any movement. For me, as a person of faith, the ground gets all the more solid when identity is found in God. My friend Candy frames it this way, "We have declared that our identity lies with Christ. That is Truth. Don't ever exchange a truth of God for a lie."

So rather than seek a group to define ourselves, we need to stay anchored in our identity based on Truth and the accompanying unique purpose and gifting individually endowed to each and

119

every one of us. Which sounds a bit Pollyannaish, since it can be so hard to do, especially when faced with finding a seat in life's proverbial cafeteria.

But the secret might be best seen in the cafeteria. Maybe part of saying no to allowing group pressures to speak into self-worth is saying hello to someone traveling alongside who needs to hear their name.

The Importance of a Name

Two things that should probably never be in the same sentence are *Kay Wyma* and *cafeteria cashier*. It has something to do with my Overtalkers Anonymous recovery program—kids waiting in a line with their food trays just wanting to pay and sit down don't have much interest in chatting—and my technological challenges.

A couple years ago, our middle school cafeteria went the way of the computer. And after having worked the lunch line in cash days when we had to do the math in our heads—let's just say I usually added a good twenty dollars at the end of my shift to help the drawer balance after all my mistakes—I'm happy for the electronic upgrade.

One of the nicest benefits of the computerized cafeteria system is that each time a student flashes their ID in order to pay for their meal from an online account, their picture and name pop up. So with every kid, I get to—by name—cheerfully yell after them, "Have a great day, Molly!" or Zack or Sam or Sally.

It's middle school, I know. They don't like to be called out or be the focus of attention, especially from a mom. But I still do it. I want them to hear their name. Said happily, positively. Sure, they might cringe on the outside, but at least for a moment, they can feel known in the sea of people. And the truth is I almost always see a faint glimmer of a smile as they walk away to find a seat.

Some of the kids even stop and shoot me back an "I hope you have a great day too."

People love to hear their name. It warms my own heart when I look up at someone who has said, "Hi, Mrs. Wyma," and I see a friend's kid smiling at me.

Dale Carnegie said, "Remember that a person's name is to that person the sweetest and most important sound in any language."[5] Why? It means you're known. And in today's world, more than ever, people need to hear their names.

Did you know that there is a World Hello Day? Yes, there is such a thing, and it is annually observed on November 21. Anyone can participate simply by greeting ten people. The goal is to demonstrate the importance of personal communication for preserving peace.

Why not use today to practice? We can say hello to the people next to us and use their names. To the grocery clerk, to the fast-food cashier, to the mailman, to someone. Just do it. And have your family do it too. A simple hello can make anyone feel a little better.

I have to confess that I am horrible at remembering people's names. I know there are tricks and tips to help me remember things like names. I even took a continuing education course at the university close to our house so I could be better at remembering names. People really matter to me—and the very least I can do is remember their names. But truth be told, I kept forgetting to even go to the class. Maybe remembering is an aptitude. One I don't have.

But even if I forget a name, God never forgets and he has promises attached to each name, for each of us.

> Do not fear, for I have redeemed you;
> > I have summoned you by name; you are mine.
> When you pass through the waters,
> > I will be with you;

and when you pass through the rivers,
    they will not sweep over you.
When you walk through the fire,
    you will not be burned;
    the flames will not set you ablaze.
For I am the LORD your God,
    the Holy One of Israel, your Savior.[6]

Everyone walks into a variety of rooms wondering where they are going to sit. Everyone sees the napkin draped over a chair and feels the sting of rejection when it is being saved for someone else or breathes a sigh of relief when it is being saved for them. But a spot at a table or in a group isn't what defines us.

Collectively, we can say no to handing over our identity and self-worth to a group. And simply knowing, trusting, and resting in the fact that sitting at a proverbial table doesn't define us, we can actually sit anywhere and with anyone. And freedom is ushered in.

When getting in my car after working in the cafeteria, I noticed a reflection of the volunteer name tag I was wearing in the window. It contains my name, printed—not handwritten upon my arrival—along with my picture. This name tag does so much more than tell someone who I am. It tells the people I pass that I belong. I'm supposed to be there.

And on that day, it acted as a reminder of the much deeper and more significant belonging, the one spoken by God that spans eternity. Why not be overwhelmed by that?

Water Station

INTERNET NICE

My grandmother would always tell us, "Say something nice, or say nothing at all." Why not take her piece of advice, go proactive, and use social media for good. Whenever Facebook Depression (yes, it's a real thing) or Instagram Envy or Pinterest Pining happens (I made the last one up) or life is handing out the blues—just say no.

Why not take matters into our own hands and overwhelm those feelings with a few good words via direct and personal messaging.

- Find a fun memory and message a childhood friend with something specific you love about them.
- Snap and send. In the carpool line the other day I was behind a mom whose young daughter literally changed princess outfits three times. She hopped out of the car to pirouette, then hopped back in for another change. Adorable. How could I not capture the moment and send it her way.
- When you see a friend share something, take a minute later in the day to send kind words her way.

A dear friend who moved across the country a couple of years ago recently Facebook messaged me:

> Hey friend . . . I was at an IF gathering tonight and I don't know why but I was struck with a memory of sitting in your living room listening to you and Jen. Just wanted you to know I miss ya!

Fond memories for me too. What a special time we shared. It was real, it was fun, and her message made me smile. Now that's some Internet Nice.

Seven

Rather Than Be Overwhelmed by Do-All Pressures, Be Overwhelmed by the Sacred in the Ordinary

My mother is a big believer in being responsible for your own happiness. She always talked about finding joy in small moments and
insisted that we stop and take in the beauty of an ordinary day.
When I stop the car to make my kids really see a sunset, I hear my
mother's voice and smile.

Jennifer Garner

"How was the basketball game?" I asked Birdie.

"Not good," he answered.

"What?" I was surprised. He and Jon had just walked in from a
game. Birdie usually has so much fun running around, shooting for
the hoop, and hanging out with his friends. "You love basketball."

"Yeah," he said thoughtfully. "I just didn't get to sit on the
bench enough."

Oh my word. Apparently, he enjoys the experience a lot more than the competition. He's never been very intense—if you can call grade-school basketball intense, though these days you probably can.

This kid—he loves life. Things that distract from the enjoyment of life can be frustrating to him. He likes to ponder and experience people, places, and things. Slow and steady set his pace. The striving part of life is a give-and-take for him. Don't get me wrong; he enjoys a challenge. But he's a lingerer, relishing regular.

Maybe some of his mentality has to do with Fury—his teenage brother who is also fairly content with being independent, specifically as it relates to the sway of public opinion or pressures. This one stays his own course, rarely compelled by what others are doing. At fifteen, he still has no cell phone. Whether you think a teenager needs a phone or not isn't the issue. The fact is almost all teenagers have a phone. But not this kid.

And it isn't because he has on-top-of-things good parents who are ever so careful to keep the evil screen world at bay. Yeah, not so much. He just doesn't want one. Truth be told, we've actually tried to push for one. Many aspects of our lives would be easier if he had a phone. It's very helpful to be able to reach your teen. And it can be a little annoying when his friends add you to their text thread because they have no way to add him. It's true. Jon is on a teenage-boy group text. He keeps taking himself off. "This is Mr. Wyma. I'm exiting the conversation."

Kind coaches have put up with our littlest guy and pushed him onward and upward—as in up off the bench. And friends have met our phoneless one where he is. Because, it would be easier for them to leave him out, but they have creatively done their best to keep him in the loop. Because people generally tend to care.

In this high-octane world that might fool us into thinking there's only one lane heading north—the fast lane—we're here to let you know that slow and steady is still around. And, quite frankly, it's not that bad. It's pretty nice. Why not let slow and steady teach us a thing or two along the way—usually to take it slow myself, to stay the course, to enjoy the scenery, and to relish in relationships rather than be distracted by loads of opportunities. Rather than be overwhelmed by all the rush to tomorrow—in whatever form is vying for our attention—why not be overwhelmed by ordinary? Relish regular so we don't forget to live today's day—so we don't miss the things that are easily overlooked, wonderful, and right in front of us.

Do-all pressures megaphone the opposite. It can be challenging to get a grip and thrive in their midst.

Busy Couture

With today's abundance of choices, it's not haute couture but busy couture that drives the high fashion of a filled calendar. We often feel we have to do all and be all in order to keep up. Filled calendar space acts as another identity definer.

In American culture, we "somehow seem to attribute higher status, higher social standing to individuals who are always busy, always working hard, always spending many hours at work," reports NPR's social science correspondent Shankar Vedantam.

"Instead of buying expensive things," Vedantam continues, "people now use busyness to show their high status. New research finds that many celebrities use social media to boast about their lack of time, not their wealth." Apparently we tend to "unconsciously conclude that busy people are also important . . . people."[1]

"Somewhere around the end of the 20th century, busyness became not just a way of life but a badge of honor," notes *Washington Post* contributor Brigid Schulte. Which is counter to Truth. "Even as neuroscience is beginning to show that at our most idle, our brains are most open to inspiration and creativity—and history proves that great works of art, philosophy and invention were

created during leisure time—we re-
sist taking time off. Psychologists
treat burned-out clients who can't
shake the notion that the busier you
are, the faster you work, and the
more you multitask, the more you
are considered competent, smart,
successful."[2]

Tricked by the do-all mantra, we
find a sort of comfort in filled spaces.
But even then contentment darts just out of reach. As soon as we
fill the spaces, human nature leads us to question, Did we choose
the right thing? Was there a better option? Am I missing something?
Should, *would*, and *could* enter the scene, and we find ourselves
trying to manage *choice anxiety*. Yes, that's a term and it can lead
to *choice paralysis*.

> The faster and busier things get, the more we need to build thinking time into our schedule. And the noisier things get, the more we need to build quiet reflection spaces in which we can truly focus.
>
> Greg McKeown[3]

Choices are supposed to be good, increased options a luxury.
But this is often not the case. Not only do we lose valuable time
researching all the options but after we make a choice, the endless options can make it harder for us to be satisfied. Thoughts
gravitate toward the ever-elusive better offer, better deal, better
activity.

"Anger at this state of affairs is comprehensible to anyone who
lives in an advanced western society . . . and has to choose between mobile phone plans, schools, and water, gas and electricity
suppliers—not to mention minimally distinguishable prospec-
tive dates," notes Stuart Jeffries of the *Guardian* as he reports on
"Why Too Much Choice Is Stressing Us Out." "Admittedly these
are the choices typical of decadent westerners in the era of late
capitalism, but that thought doesn't make the burden of choice
any easier to bear."[4]

Then, in the strangest way, rather than sigh in relief after making
a choice, our natural inclination to doubt is further exasperated by

127

expectations that accompany choices. We have what seems a natural impression "that life choices we made after careful planning should bring us expected results—happiness, security, contentment—and that with better choices, traumatic feelings that we have when dealing with loss, risk and uncertainty can be avoided," says Professor Renata Salecl, author of *The Tyranny of Choice*. Such an attitude can take the overwhelming nature of choice overload to a new level. "When people are overwhelmed by choice and when they are anxious about it, they often turn to denial, ignorance and willful blindness."[5]

This is the place where we can say no. Giving in to society's do-all pressures leads to a proverbial grave rather than abundant life. And these pressures simply are not the boss of us.

Rather than be overwhelmed by do-all pressures, why not reach for ordinary? Though that word might evoke visions of boredom and possibly ignite embers of fear—as in the fear of being left out, left behind, and unseen—it falls in the category of counterintuitive abundance.

What does it look like? Mostly like things that can get classified as unproductive since tangible is rarely on the other side of boring—because that tends to be slow.

The Sacred in the Ordinary

For the most part, days are ordinary. My sister-in-law said it well one day when we were doing what we do—phone chat. We touch base often.

Not long ago she was filling me in on her exciting times in Atlanta: a trip to Costco, taking a kid to tennis, rearranging her house. She's always switching things around. And in the switching she started to get excited about having Thanksgiving at her house. So she decided to look for a few fall decorations while she was out running errands.

Apparently, such decor was hard to find in September. Christmas—yes. Fall—not so much.

And she thought about how often in the rush we miss out on some of the good. And then she thought about all the good that can be found in the ordinary—the ordinary we live every day.

"There's sacred in the ordinary," she said. "We get ready every day. We run the dishwasher every day. We drive to the same places. We fold and put away the laundry. And then we do it all again the next day. We live regular life that is on the whole ordinary."

She continued and tied the bow: "All the retail Christmas onslaught and my effort to find Thanksgiving in the midst of it made me think. Seriously, I had to search in the store to find anything autumn related. It made me think about not rushing today to get to tomorrow, to live in the day, to enjoy it. Otherwise I will miss it. It will be gone, and I'll look back and wonder what I was doing."

There you have it. When aisle upon aisle of Christmas decorations in September make us feel as if we're way behind or that we must stick our toe into the maddening rush so that we don't miss out, we say no. Because it's actually in the trying not to miss out that we so often do.

There is sacred in the ordinary.

Ordinary is saying hi to the cafeteria worker or the drive-through guy. Sacred is the connection that occurs when a name is said.

Ordinary is a quick dash to the grocery store. Sacred is the personal encounter that occurs when we bump into someone in the frozen food aisle whom we haven't seen in a while. It's helping a stranger who needs assistance or a kind word, since it's highly likely they encountered unnecessary rudeness in the parking lot vying for a spot.

Ordinary is obligatorily walking outside with a kid because he doesn't want to go down the block by himself to take pictures or collect things for a school project. Sacred is when that kid stops to point out the tiniest place where sunlight has peeked through a tree's leaves to shine directly on a small butterfly balancing on a blade of grass.

Ordinary is picking up clothes lying directly in front of the laundry hamper almost every day—as if those responsible can't just open the door and put them inside. Ordinary is fighting feelings of frustration at the audacity of such actions and the implied superiority they bring with them. Sacred is the chance to see beyond those clothes—to embrace opportunities to serve, to gently remind those walking alongside us how inadvertent actions affect others, to be thankful for a life filled with relationship in all its good and bad, its ups and downs.

Many opportunities to see the sacred in the ordinary present themselves every day. Is it possible to see them all? Probably not. But catching a few glimpses might help us say no to do-all pressures and help us slow down so we don't forget to live today's day.

After all, we might miss something wonderful in the rush for tomorrow.

"I love fall," my sister-in-law continued. "The leaves changing colors is beyond beautiful. I guess I just don't want to let induced-rush by retailers take away from the beauty of today."

Me neither.

Watch the leaves turn color and sink into all that comes with fall and the amazing holiday it hosts. Relish the beauty before the starkness of winter sets in. Then let the seasonal days bring with them a beauty of their own.

Why let the rush distract us? All the do-all pressures don't get to crowd out today. They are not the boss of us. Today has merit and can be lived and enjoyed.

In the time ambush, remember this: we're not behind, even though the back-to-school season or holidays or life expectations attempt to make us think we are. And when we're bombarded by the do-all pressures, why not stop and be thankful.

Practicing thankfulness holds back temptation by all the options. We can instead focus with gratitude on all we already have rather than on what we could, would, or should have. We can be

"The trees that are slow to grow, bear the best fruit."

—Molière

Slow down. Go through the process. Continue on your journey even if it is the scenic route. The time you reach your destination is *not* the most important thing. The journey, the learning experience, and your growth are most important. Many times the slow journey will produce the best results *in us*.

Jackie Bledsoe[6]

thankful for the house we have rather than let it say anything about us or our self-worth. We can celebrate with friends who jet from event to event rather than give in to a notion that we're not doing enough. Gratitude is our hydration, and it centers on recognizing and being thankful to God for his perfect provision.

We can inhale thankfulness that acts as a reminder of ordinary's abundance. Then exhale stress and pressures that would lead us to think otherwise.

A Sacred Sighting

"Mom, where *are* you?" Barton texted. She'd been waiting for me to pick her up from school.

Usually she drives herself and Fury, but not these days.

A few weeks earlier, she had been dog sitting again. Three times a day, she headed to Nike's where she would feed him, take him on walks, and as of late, simply hang out. Anytime she gets to be with a dog, she lingers. And since she'd set a goal for herself to read thirty-five books in a year, reading with a pup snuggled up close sounded wonderful.

Off she went, book in hand, one last time for the day before Nike's owners got home. As she was pulling into their drive, a car coming up from behind plowed into the side end of Barton's car. The impact was so powerful it spun her all the way to the left where she ended facing the other car's driver. He looked at her, backed up his car, then pulled forward to speed off. A hit and run.

The bad part of the accident was a crunched car and a bruised psyche—it still boggles my mind that the other driver had the audacity to speed away. The good part? No injuries and the kids were back in the car with me. For me, with every trip to the DMV to encourage a nervous sixteen-year-old with the same "you can do this" they've heard and endured over the years, my heart breaks a little. I know all too well that the days of them sitting close to me are quickly coming to an end. Needless to say, the riding with me result made me happy. Even though my tardiness might not make it look that way.

"I'm late," I replied. "Be there in five to ten." The kids are accustomed to waiting. It comes with the territory of a large family.

When I finally arrived, I braced myself for a legitimate "What took you so long?" Especially since the day brought with it gusty cold winds as she stood outside. But that's not at all what got in the car.

"I just experienced the sweetest thing," Barton excitedly said. "Oh my gosh. Okay, so I was standing on the corner waiting—and waiting—and waiting," she smirked, needing to get in at least one dig. "And all of a sudden a man turned down the street the wrong way. A lady kind of honked at him—not loud. He looked at me and I pointed at the One Way sign, so he quickly turned into a drive so he could park. He was adorable."

She took a breath and continued. "So he got out of his car and came right toward me and told me he liked my sweatshirt." She was wearing her Camp Barnabas—a camp in Northern Arkansas for folks with special needs—shirt. "He said 'I live right down the street from Camp Barnabas. It sure is a special place.' We talked about that for a minute. I told him I worked there last summer. Then he asked me if I knew his granddaughter and that he was there to pick her up. I don't know her well, but I know who she is. So I told him yes and how nice she is. Then, he saw her coming out of the school, told me how nice it was to chat and turned to walk and meet her."

She took another breath, I could almost feel her happiness. "That's when the *cutest* thing happened. As she got closer to him, he took off his coat and wrapped her in it with the hugest hug. It was *so* cute. Oh my word, he's so nice. You could tell how much he loves her. And how sweet for him to know she might be cold and that her being warm mattered to him more than his being warm. Oh my goodness."

Rather than be frustrated with me for being late, rather than be crabby because she was freezing from standing on the corner for so long, and rather than be overwhelmed by the colossal amount of schoolwork about to fill her afternoon and evening, she relished in every second of something she found beautiful. A very sacred moment in the ordinary.

If she had been looking down or if her eyes had been anchored on herself with all that could have legitimately warranted some being put out, she never would have seen such a beautiful picture of love.

The neatest thing about the scene was that it kept informing her afternoon. More than once she came back to me, "He was just so nice. And how sweet to give her his coat. Oh . . . so cute."

I wondered if she knew how regular it was for a grandpa or dad to take off his coat and give it to his girl. There was nothing regular about his gesture to her. That brief interaction in front of the high school was sacred. And that sacred moment lasted a long time. Something so small and so simple overwhelmed a young lady and breathed life into her day. Simply because she was looking and engaged.

Are these moments occurring all the time? All around us? Maybe. Why not practice today finding sacred in the ordinary—or seeing and recognizing the beauty and wonder of regular that surrounds us each and every day?

Water Station

PRACTICE THANKFULNESS

The opportunity to practice thankfulness seems to have no boundaries, even though it is often overlooked. Not only do opportunities amply avail themselves, scientifically documented benefits come along for the ride.

Amy Morrin shares seven benefits of gratitude in *Forbes* magazine.

- Gratitude opens the door to more relationships.
- Gratitude improves physical health.
- Gratitude improves psychological health. "Grateful people experience fewer aches and pains and they report feeling healthier than other people."
- Gratitude enhances empathy and reduces aggression.
- Grateful people sleep better.
- Gratitude improves self-esteem.
- Gratitude increases mental strength.[7]

So why not practice today so we can be hydrated for days when we might struggle?

Find something nice to say and say it—specifically. Maybe we can go one step farther and find a way to thank a hard-to-love person in our life. You never know what might be on the other side of that.

A simple thank-you with no expectations of one in return can be just the gentle word that someone needs to hear.

Be grateful today so tomorrow's long lines and traffic and all that comes with it won't get our blood boiling.

As if on considering-thankfulness-cue, Birdie, our commercial-kid—as in, "I've got to buy the toy they just advertised"—got in the car after school.

"Do you know about gravity?" he asked me.

"Yes . . . ," I replied, wondering where he was going.

"Well, earth has gravity," he said. "It's weird, isn't it? What if it pushed out instead of pulling in?"

"That wouldn't be good," I replied.

"No," he said in all his elementary-school contemplation which ended with the conclusion, "it would absolutely not be good—we'd fall off." Then he added, "I'll tell you one thing I'm grateful for—gravity. I don't think I'd like much of anything that would come with falling off the earth."

So yes, all day every day, every one of us has something for which to be grateful. Let's hope that as we practice thankfulness we can see something every day for which to be grateful. But if not, why not take Birdie's lead and land on gravity.

eight

Rather Than Be Overwhelmed by Product Pressures, Be Overwhelmed by the Process

Transformation is a process, and as life happens there are tons of ups and downs. It's a journey of discovery—there are moments on mountaintops and moments in deep valleys of despair.

Rick Warren

Required summer reading is one of those things I don't think I will miss when the last of our crew holds a high school diploma in his hand. The requirement aspect of such tasks kind of ruins their potential. But what if we invited all the wonder and beauty woven with a process to overwhelm us rather than the duty, the enormity, or even the mundane that accompanies tasks?

I remember my own relationship with summer-reading re-quirements. The first book I ever had to read for school during the summer was *The Hobbit* in a year when I switched schools. Up to that point, I had never heard of a summer-reading requirement.

Honestly, being a reader, I was excited to have a new book in my hands. Until I learned there would be a test on it. That kind of wrecked the fun and made it a task.

I wrestled with the questions and expectations and stress, knowing that the grade I would receive on the test would be my first grade in a new school and would likely set the stage for how my teacher would regard me as a student. It was overwhelming.

What started as something fun quickly turned into a sour drudgery. Once in a while I'd catch myself enjoying Tolkien's story until I remembered that reading it was a task.

So I get it. I know and understand that a lot of the wonder that could accompany a task such as summer reading gets lost in the completion of it. Things like required reading tend to be done rather than savored, which equals product over process.

The books my kids have on deck this year are actually terrific. Each of them, in their unique genres, has something to offer any reader. I picked up one of them, *The Sufferings of Young Werther*—a book I had never heard of until seeing it on a kid's bed. I figured if a knowledgeable teacher who lives for literature chose it as required reading, it must be something worthwhile. Before long, I found myself annotating. Granted, I'm a complete geek, but it's a good book—like most of them must be. I've even had to order that kid another copy since I decided to keep his.

But will he savor it the way I am? Will he be able to move beyond the task to enjoy the process? Doubtful. Truth be told, I've sat next to three kids reading George MacDonald's *The Princess and the Goblin* with the biggest grumbler being me. In fact, I was the one leading the not-again, not-this-book charge until the last reading with Birdie. For whatever reason, I joined rather than berated him and read the amazing story that many months later I'm still savoring.

Summer reading, at the onset, was never meant to be a checked box. The impetus was simply to keep kids involved, to promote brain exercise during time away from formal learning. But here's where we can witness up close and personal the issue of making a task about completion rather than the process. Because we do this in all sorts of ways throughout life.

If my kids read a book to complete a requirement—performance based on an audience made up of their teacher and their peers—then they don't get much out of it.

But if by some chance one of them picks up a book, reads it, wrestles with it, and goes so far as to consider the meaning behind the writing, there is a high likelihood that something of great value might occur in the process.

So I wonder, what else is being lost in our obsession with product? We have countless tasks to accomplish that added together supposedly get us to where we need to be. So why don't they?

Product pressures exist and can even be important when they inspire excellence, but if given too much ground, they can easily overwhelm and completely suck the joy out of the process.

And, dare we consider product pressures as they relate to people? We can easily have product pressures in our relationships—because relationships are "supposed to" look a certain way. (See also: marriage, family, friendships.)

In education, we've become so driven by blue-ribbon and top-tier lists that the love of learning has gotten lost along the way, shoved behind loads of good intentions and pressures to land at a certain number in order to qualify for funding.

In politics, we are slaves to instant polling and public opinion, and we have lost decorum and leadership. We have lost sight of relationships that form as people join forces to forge the way together or as they disagree and work through differences in order to land on common ground. That process is slow and can be messy.

Product pressures might be the fiercest when it comes to raising kids, probably because we care so deeply about our kids. Sure, we strive to do well in other areas, but we desperately want our kids to turn out okay. And blinded by such hope, we can lose sight of the process in our efforts to get to the product. But, again, people aren't a product, although the résumé race might claim otherwise.

In my world, we're swimming upstream against the college application current. I don't want my kids' lives to be about a résumé, but society lures us to believe that's what matters. We herald the résumé: community service—"for the hours," rather than the joy of serving; summer jobs—"show initiative"; clubs— "communicate well-roundedness"; athletics—"show that you're a team player"; and so on.

It is a game. It must be played. Which is fine as long as we don't completely sacrifice the process for the product—let alone the person.

So as I watch and chide, I wonder, will my kids finish the task of churning through hundreds of pages so they can check a box? Or might they, just for a moment, enjoy the process and learn something? Might they play on a team, join a club, serve in the community simply for the experience?

Producing is overwhelming at best. The process just might be where joy resides.

Stress Bombs

"My high school counselor told me that if I didn't take three years of language, I would likely get passed over by colleges because the application next to mine would look better," Matt told me. Matt is one of our kids' small group leaders. He is an accomplished musician who got into and attended the University of North Texas, known around the world for its College of Music, specifically its jazz specialty.

"I listened," he continued, "and did what my advisor told me. I took the extra year of Spanish to look good for colleges instead of the woodwinds elective that I wanted to take. And you know," he concluded, now in his twenties and able to look back, "I would have been fine without the Spanish. And I'm not sure that third year had any bearing on my college acceptances. I can't help but look back and wonder why I let the stress of college acceptance play such a big role. I let the pressures win out over what I loved."

I call this the college bomb.

Parents, advisors, coaches, and the like—all of whom are well meaning—tend to play the stress bomb card. And it can be lobbed as early as grade school, even by friends.

This scenario played out in my backseat the other day amid a group of ten-year-olds.

"Are you doing Boy Scouts?" a friend asked Birdie.

"I don't know," he replied. "Don't Boy Scouts pick up trash on the side of the road?"

Oh my word, I thought. *We've got to clue him in.*

"No," Boy Scout kid replied.

"You know, colleges look at stuff like Boy Scouts," another added.

"Yeah, you won't get in without circulars."

What? They're ten. He doesn't even know the word, but he knows that extracurriculars matter. Why are the pressures raised so early? Can't they have fun? Participate in Boy Scouts because they like camping, learning, being outside, fixing things?

Our freshman in college—with the college bomb behind her—is now experiencing similar life-determining pressures related to choosing a major that will lead to a job. And such pressures are the topic of conversation around every corner. What are you studying? What do you want to do with your life? Legitimate questions lobbed by kind folks who have likely forgotten the stress of college, since they deal with different pressures in their own life stages. Because stress bombs appear throughout life.

For kids—and parents—the college bomb is big. But as soon as that has been cleared, the job bomb is right around the corner.

Then there's the multifaceted status bomb that loves to wreak havoc throughout life: married/not married, job/no job, title/no title, babies/no babies, homeowner/renter, etc.

Stress bombs tend to produce strong feelings of inadequacy and evoke fear—as in fear of failure, fear of being behind, fear of being left out or completely out of touch. Usually a sense of anxiety joins the party and overstays its welcome. It brings with it all sorts of what-ifs known to knock even the most well balanced off their game. Which inevitably evokes self-questioning, self-doubt, and scrambling.

As we are discovering, the college bomb lingers and makes things such as class selection less about the person and their purpose and more about product.

All stress bombs take the joy out of the task at hand and make it about performing rather than learning and enjoying the process part. The process is one of the best parts of life.

The Process over the Product

Life's product pressures make me angry. I'm guessing they affected B. Decimal point numbers in a GPA easily captivate thoughts and inform self-worth. I find it a challenge to walk in the halls that whispered such messaging to B—the halls that my kids and hundreds of others walk every day. I literally want to scream to each human being on their way to classes or *circulars*, "Don't listen!"

But the truth is numbers do have a voice in choices and decisions. Product pressures are like storms we must weather in order to make it to the other side. To be able to live within the pressures yet never allow them to overwhelm us and have the final say is the challenge.

I thought about the process when playing cards with Fury. Rummy to be exact. Our version of Rummy is like Gin Rummy, but with a bit more strategy and gamesmanship. One hand doesn't make the game. And you can play off each other's hands. The discard pile stays alive, and points are gained or lost based on cards laid less those remaining in a hand. We usually play to five hundred.

Of late, the game had been especially fun since one of the kids had caught the Rummy bug. Well, mostly fun. Sometimes he can get frustrated.

"Did you shuffle?" Fury asked, slightly perturbed as he looked at what he thought was a less-than-winning hand.

"Yes," I replied. "You watched me."

He eyed me suspiciously. I ignored him.

It was my turn to go first, and I did something that was sure to fire up his ire. I began the game by laying down points.

"What?" he protested. "That's not fair." He eyed the cards I'd played and questioned, "You had those in your hand?"

What could I do but admit, "I was dealt a great hand."

"That's not fair!" he protested again. "My hand is terrible." Then he went down the pity road. "I'm going to lose. That's all there is to it. I'm losing for sure."

"You know that's not true." I tried to offer perspective, tried to remind him that it was a game, a game that involves more than one hand, that what he held in his current hand didn't define him. You know, all that mom stuff that sounds like squirrel chatter. Yes, this was a game of cards, but I can sometimes have a hard time hearing those perspective words in the game of life.

"There are lots of cards to play," I encouraged him to think beyond the moment. But he wanted nothing to do with it. He was dying to know my hand and to lament even further the unfairness of it all.

"What else do you have," he asked. "I bet you have the aces too."

"Oh my word." I shook my head. "You had a great hand last time. Can't you be happy for me this time?"

"We need to start over," he declared. "My hand is terrible. It's the worst hand ever!"

We did not start over. We played that hand—which he lost—and more. At the end of it all, he ended with more points than I did, winning. Even though such a prospect looked dim at the beginning.

It's a little like life, isn't it? And it can happen at any stage. We start something like a new school year or a new job or a new project, and we eye each other's cards, thinking about all the I'm-so-glad-I-gots or wallowing in the I-wish-I-hads. Someone got the teacher our child wanted. The other project is a slam dunk, while ours will for sure be a legal nightmare. My kid should have made the A team or be sitting in the front of the room. Or maybe we have a terrific a set of circumstances, for the moment—everything for which we hoped.

But like the game of Rummy, life is long. It isn't all about one set of circumstances—the things that simply happen. It doesn't end with the first play. Life is so much more than a single project or a single semester or a single year. It's made up of multiple plays that work together to make a whole. Still, we try to position ourselves to have the best, to be the best. And it's often hard to rest with the cards in our hand. Because somewhere along the way we begin to think that the hand defines us.

And with that in mind, we can't help but wonder, *What's in their hand? What if that card is an ace?* We worry about what everyone else has. And the agony of not knowing makes us want to know even more, mostly so we can be sure we're okay.

If our set of circumstances declares our relevancy and worth, then how can we not help but allow it to define us? But unlike a game of cards, which truly hinges on luck and timing, life never relies on luck.

This is where knowing God came into the picture for me. Perspective and trust are keys to seeing beyond the product pressures and circumstances—both bad and good. God knows each and every hand that is dealt. And he is Lord over all the timing.

Is it fair to compare life to a card game? Probably not. But I'm tired of there being a right way; I'm tired of the pressure to strive; I'm tired of all the endless spin and positioning. Why not be overwhelmed by, sink into, and linger in the process with all its highs and lows loaded with experience. The process is okay, even good, but it banks on trust—a hard thing when all you can see is the hand you've been dealt.

Long View

[People] are prone to focus on the negatives. You kind of blow off the positives unless it's something particularly spectacular.

But even there, you have a certain achievement and almost immediately feel the pressure of doing it again. It's almost a trap.

And so, reminding students in particular that it's more about the process than the result is important.

Sometimes drawing a parallel to sports helps me because it's a lot more physical and I can see it. Think about a ten-year-old who is shooting a basketball into a ten-foot goal and how awkward that looks. Often kids are more successful when they shoot in unorthodox ways—as in underhand.

But they're developing the wrong habit. And over time, it's actually more beneficial for them to miss a lot right now. Because as they get bigger, their success rate is going to develop as they grow. And they will actually be better prepared in the long run if they miss more now.

The same is true in lots of other areas—it's just not quite so obvious.

The longer you go at something and the more you see the end result pay off, the more confidence you have in the process. But there is always this lingering fear or doubt that it's worked before, but is it going to work again this time? . . . And I really think that's where prayer comes into the picture.

Trusting the Process

I guess for me, if God is involved in the answer to Life's Over-whelmed—as I found myself convinced and saying out loud that day so many years ago when I quit buying into the world's messaging that had led to an eating disorder—then I'd like to know him better, to understand him on a deeper level so that trust becomes my go-to rather than the trappings of this world.

Without trust in a sovereign God who is authoring our story, you are prone to fear. But knowing that he can redeem even bad things is sort of the hope that I return to often—to just help me to trust and push forward and keep going. I could tell you many stories of kids whose parents were, you know, pulling their hair out and wondering "What are we going to do?" But within two or three years, [they] look back and think, "Wow, what a transformation! We kept with the process and look what resulted. I'm so glad we did."

I think a lot of it comes from trying to see the long view, rather than giving in to the moment. Long-term view, sticking with the process even when fear enters the picture.

I was having a conversation with some new faculty about mak-ing too much of a comparison at a particular moment particularly in a child's development and we were talking about reading. And I asked, "How many of you were reading before you were four? How many of you were reading not until you were six and a half?" And then we all kind of had a laugh because who cares?

But in a given moment we tend to make a lot of it—like it's going to affect where a child ends up or set them on course for the rest of their life. Development happens at different speeds for different people. But we're all going to get there.

The more that [we] can have that healthy view, the more that will be transmitted to the child and they will be able to roll with the punches.

Jeff Hendricks, headmaster of Providence Christian School[1]

In the Bible, story after story records history, ancient history, the story of people who lived on this planet and dealt with pretty much the same things we deal with today, just wrapped in different packaging.

It can be easy to lose sight of the countless hours, days, and years of simply regular mundane life that pass from Genesis to Revelation—many of those years were full of very regular mundane. For example, before facing the giant Goliath in an epic battle during the eleventh century BC, David spent years tending sheep—far from glamour. But did that process ever pay off? While tending sheep, vigilantly guarding the group day after day and year after year, David honed his skill using a sling.

Malcom Gladwell in his book *David and Goliath: Underdogs, Misfits, and the Art of Battling Giants* shares some insights on the famous interaction. In ancient times there were three kinds of warriors: cavalry, foot soldiers, and projectile warriors—or artillery—the last of which included archers and slingers.

> Slingers had a leather pouch attached on two sides by a long strand of rope. They would put a rock or a lead ball into the pouch, swing it around in increasingly wider and faster circles, and then release one end of rope, hurling the rock forward.
>
> Slinging took an extraordinary amount of skill and practice. When [David] tells Saul that he has killed bears and lions as a shepherd, he does so not just as testimony to his courage but to make another point as well: that he intends to fight Goliath the same way he has learned to fight wild animals—as a projectile warrior.[2]

David practiced in those long hours caring for and protecting his family's flock while his older brothers were off at war. Clearly he didn't shy away from the tedium of the process but used time and process to gain expertise. He didn't take shortcuts or become distracted by what his brothers were doing—engaging in a much worthier effort, according to societal standards of his day—but rather David stayed his course. How could he have known that all he learned while embracing his lot would be utilized at a later date when he would use his combat skills to lead a band of warriors and his shepherding skills to lead a kingdom?

But not every process ends with slaying a giant or becoming king.

Jonathan, the son of King Saul, had a very different path to travel. Jonathan, by all logic and standards, should have been holding David's cards. Jonathan, heir apparent, was the commander of the army, a well-respected, wise, and rightly celebrated leader. He was trustworthy and cared deeply for the men under his command as well as the people with whom they crossed paths.

But the king card was never his to play.

Yet he was happy. His joy wasn't sapped. He even celebrated his young friend who would be king. Not only did Jonathan celebrate David, he mentored and cheered for him from the sidelines. How could he do that? He should have been king.

Both David and Jonathan considered their path in the context of trusting God's plan, embracing the path and the process rather than the product. Which, in a compelling way, allowed each to fully develop the skills they needed for each of their purposes—one as anointed king and the other as mentor and encourager—alongside each other, together.

Such trust allowed Jonathan to care for and encourage those around him rather than be consumed by what could easily be deemed unfair. He knew that getting ahead or winning or being better, maybe even the best (as the world defines best), didn't offer peace. It was in serving, accepting, embracing, and doing his best with his life and purpose that he found peace.

But how does that work for us today?

We won't always know which is the right path to follow. Regardless, we put one foot in front of the other, weighing out the decisions and actions that line the path, eyes anchored on Truth rather than on culture's shifting ways and standards.

Why not remember—in the midst of college acceptances/ rejections, sorority bids/cuts, making the A team or the C team, party invitations or lack thereof, pregnancies or miscarriages, job offers or cuts, diagnoses, and so much more—to consider the bigger picture and to trust. Maybe then we can enjoy the process rather than make it about the product—and in turn, peace.

The process matters—because people matter. People are not products—more like works in process with the process being each person's story. Rather than be overwhelmed by product pressures, why not be overwhelmed by the process which brings back into the picture the humanness of life—the ups and downs, the highs and lows that make a life.

Water Station

MAKE A LIST AND CHECK IT TWICE

"It can be hard not only *seeing* all the people that make life look easy but when I watch E struggle," my sweet friend Beth honestly shares, "I can barely *not* make it about me. As if her failure is my fault. When she didn't make the cut, it was my fault—at least in my head. All the *should've*s ran through iterations of what I could have done to help her hit the marks I think need hitting. And I tanked. It is so overwhelming."

She's right.

"Maybe it's all those performance reviews that make me apply the same system to my parenting. Which is slightly ridiculous since kids are people. And I know it's wrong, because I don't believe those messages to be true. But I just can't stop myself."

So I ask because I want to know, "What do you do, to get out of the funk? Like practically?"

Then she hits me with a couple terrific hands-on approaches to reframe Overwhelmed.

Try to Turn a Negative into a Positive

"Well, when E didn't make the team, we talked about how that doesn't define her. I think I was telling myself as much as her. Then we sat down together and used the Cricut to make little volleyballs and wrote the girls', names on them for their lockers. E loves crafts so it got her out of the funk, made the other girls happy, and took a topic they would likely avoid—so as not to hurt E's feelings but would have made her feel left out—and brought it out into the open. It worked. Doesn't always, but it did then."

"And serving others," she added. "Getting out of your own head often gives you a different perspective on your situation. Serving others can break your cycle of fear and worry and anxiety because you are focusing on someone other than yourself."

Write Out Life's Overwhelmed and Truth That Puts It in Its Place

"Then," she continued, "for myself when I'm dealing with thoughts—like fears that quickly become too much—I make a list. I write a list of whatever has made it hard to breathe, then next to it I write Truth.

"For instance, since E didn't make the team, my fear is that she'll be left out or that she'll feel like a failure which will in turn spill into other areas of her life. What if she's then left out or alone? And so on. I write these things down, then next to it I try to write a Truth that informs that fear. Like, 'She is not alone. God sees her.' God created her, he made her super creative and artsy, maybe not the best athlete. That she has survived other things and is okay. Those written reminders almost instantly bring peace in the midst of what minutes earlier was perched, ready to take me down."

Powerful perspective saves the day.

"There's something about writing it down that helps me."

I believe she's right about that. We feel it when writing, see it when reading, and if we say it out loud, there's definitely hearing going on and possibly taste. The last might be a stretch, but it sure involves a lot of our senses.

> Impressions gained through your senses are crucial for your memory. The more of your senses sight, hearing, taste, touch and smell you can use, the more fields in the brain you use, and the more vividly you can remember.[3]

Phone a Friend

"Well, talking helps. I'm glad you called," she said.

"Listen," I reply. "Everything you've said has helped *me*!" She *had* been on my mind, I stuffed the usual *I don't want to bother her, she's probably busy* objections, and I called to say hi.

Seriously. We are not alone in any of life—the good, the bad, the easy, and the hard. None of us has all the answers. Maybe we aren't supposed to. But we can share and encourage each other. Safe friendships made all the greater by open and honest conversation. Walking life together.

nine

Rather Than Be Overwhelmed by Circumstances, Be Overwhelmed by Looking Up

Since the birds have learned so well the art of trusting Him and of casting their cares from themselves upon God, we who are His children should do so even more.

Martin Luther

Opening the cupboard to see two boxes of coffee K-Cups completely empty at 8:45 p.m. the night before a morning gathering at my house can be a bit deflating, let alone slightly overwhelming as I had nary a minute to get coffee for myself in the first place that day.

I wanted to point fingers and lecture, *My word, people, why put an empty box back on the shelf? There's a new invention called the trash can. Empty items go there to be discarded. Oh, and another crazy thing? With the box gone, it's easy to know we're out and need more. Really. How hard can it be?*

151

I know the lecture because I might have given it the other day when I noticed that of the eight boxes of cereal on the shelf in our pantry, six had less than an eighth of an inch of cereal left in them. I think it fell on deaf ears. There may have been listening but not much on the hearing part.

But on this particular evening, my little soliloquy, though lovely and inspiring, would have been directed toward only one person—me. I'm the only one who drinks coffee. Apparently, *I* left the empty boxes. Guess the apples don't fall too far from the tree.

The empty-box discovery came at the end of a rough day. People say that a mom is only as happy as her least happy child. And I had a sad one that day. The house was a bit of a wreck—with seven regular people living in it, there's only so much space for all the regular stuff. The multifaceted stress coupled with the next day's early morning gathering made those empty boxes even more frustrating. Couldn't one thing be easy? Apparently, not today. And to top it all off, the store that sold K-Cups didn't open until nine the next morning, which is when people were coming.

Barton, diligently working away on an art project, noticed my deep sigh. "What's wrong?"

"Oh, nothing," I replied. "I just thought I'd get a jump on tomorrow and do a little setting up for the meeting, but we're out of coffee. It's completely my fault, but I'm a bit bummed."

"I'm sorry." So sweet, she really was. "Hey, I bet you can make it to the store before it closes. It's only 8:45," she encouraged, then saw something in the stack of mail next to her on the counter. "And here are a couple of coupons!"

Well, there you have it. With a little wind in my sail and coupons in my hand, I raced out the door on my way to Bed, Bath & Beyond.

Sure enough, I got there with three minutes to spare. I grabbed a cart and made my way through the crowd—no one was there—to the back of the store and perused all the choices, making sure to grab a few more than I needed so I wouldn't be staring at empty boxes again soon.

Heading to the checkout, I was thankful for a kid who cared enough to help solve a problem. I loved that she didn't let me allow a minor situation after a long day be bigger than it should be. I was even thankful for the walk out of the house and into the store. I was filled with fresh air and able to glimpse a beautiful dark sky dotted with bright stars. I think I needed a bit of a breather. Who knew that a quick sprint to the store would be just that? Barton had helped me be overwhelmed by nighttime serenity through looking up.

The only other people in the store, besides the security guard and employees, were checking out in front of me. Two older ladies—the shopper and her friend—were discussing what they could buy. The shopper rummaged through her items, trying to figure out what to keep and what to put back. I didn't think much about it, figuring that maybe they, like I so often do, had come to the store without the right card or with too little cash.

They were so cute figuring it all out while the cashier waited patiently.

Having had the evening's fresh air breathe some life into my very long day, I certainly wasn't in a hurry. I enjoyed watching them move things from one cart to the other, then back again. That's about the time I realized that all the moving of items had to do with coupons—of which they didn't have enough.

I looked at their carts, filled with mostly large items. Then I looked at my cart, sparse with boxes of coffee, and quickly deduced (since I'm so quick at math—not!) that my 20 percent off coupons would get them a lot farther than they would me. So I joined their conversation. Something I'm known to do.

"Is it a coupon issue?" I asked, nodding at the carts.

"What?" the lady pushing the cart looked back and asked.

"Oh, I don't mean to intrude"—my kids would disagree—"but if you need another coupon, I have a couple."

"What?" she asked again, this time in a more "you'd do that" sort of way.

"Well, they're yours if you'll have them. I mean, look at my stuff—it's all little. The coupons will have a bigger impact on your bill than mine."

Both of the ladies burst out, "Laahwd have mercy" as they poked each other and shook their heads.

I was slightly taken aback, as was the cashier.

"You're giving me your coupons?" she asked again.

"Well, yeah."

Then they both died laughing, the happiest laugh, a can-you-believe-our-luck sort of laugh. At which point I shrugged and started laughing too. I guess laughter actually is contagious.

Then church started.

"Oh, Jesus. Thank you, Jesus," the shopper started to say with her hands lifted up. She turned to me. "Honey, you have no idea. I came in here to get these goods. A couple are for me, but most are for a friend from church who has hit the bottom."

Then her friend joined. "We thought we brought all our coupons, but somewhere we dropped 'em or lost 'em or I don't know— we just don't have 'em all."

Then back to the other. "And here you come, right out of the blue with the coupons we need. Like manna from heaven. Exactly what we need shows right up with you." Then she lifted her hands, and they shouted/sang, "Praise Jesus! Mighty Savior! God Provider!"

The stunned cashier was looking on.

I felt like I was in a religious Publisher's Clearing House commercial, waiting for balloons to fall and a guy with a ginormous check to pop up from behind the other cash register. The security guard was smiling ear to ear, nodding and shaking his head, kind of raising his hands at the same time. And I thought to myself, *Provider is one of God's names—Jehovah Jireh.*

They were just a couple of coupons.

But not to them. I guess, by this point, not to me either.

"Honey, what is your name?" the lady ardently asked me.

"Kay."

Then the two screamed, "What! Your name is *Kay*?" Then they addressed the security guard. "Her name is *Kay*!"

The friend nodded at me and pointed to the lady pushing the cart. "Her name is Kay too."

"Seriously?" I asked. Kay is not the most popular name around town. "Wow, that's kind of crazy," I replied as I handed her my coupons. "I can't tell you how so very happy I am for you to have these. And how grateful I am." I went on to explain, "I was having such a bad day—a day I thought couldn't get any worse. At least until I opened a kitchen cabinet and saw empty boxes of coffee. I was so frustrated and felt like quitting. The only reason I needed coffee was to make tomorrow morning nice for some ladies coming to my house. Then my daughter handed me the coupons and so nicely encouraged me to run over here. And who knew? My word, so special."

Then the cashier weighed in with a smirky smile. "You just never know, do you?" Then he looked at me and said, "I've got coupons for you. You're covered."

"What?"

"It's my pleasure to pay your kindness forward, right back to you."

"You don't have to do that," I tried to protest.

"Of course I don't," he replied. "I want to."

"My goodness, thank you so much," I said.

The ladies were loving every minute.

Then the cashier nodded at all of us. "My name is Ray."

We died laughing. Hilarious. Kay, Kay, and Ray.

As he was ringing up my stuff, I told him, "When I was in grade school, I often had teachers call me Ray. My cursive capital *K* looked a bit more like an *R* than a *K*, so I was often Ray."

We all laughed some more—and we relished.

The Kays had been shaking their heads earlier, feeling like they were coming up short, possibly questioning what else could happen, thinking they had nothing left to give.

But things weren't short at all. They were covered.

I wondered as I made my way to the car, my heart literally bursting from the fullness, whether I would have been able to experience such a special experience if my eyes had been down, glued to the moment.

I'm so thankful that my eyes were looking up. And thankful that Barton is traveling alongside me.

What a sweet, special, memorable reminder—on any day, but especially on hard ones.

Life's Overwhelmed had been arrested. It tried to ride the coattails of a long day, but it didn't succeed. Since we've started our trek to call out Overwhelmed and put it in its place, we've experienced so much freedom. And we've learned that we often need each other to be able to see beyond a moment. And we need encouragement, which is what Barton gave me.

Walking out of the house to try and make it to the store before it closed, I breathed fresh air. The small act of exercise outside to and from the car on my street and in a store parking lot acted like a cool drink of water and helped clear my mind so thoughts could refresh. Then some ordinary shopping turned sacred and overwhelmed not only me but everyone in its sphere—all spurred by looking up beyond the moment. Something to remember when days turn especially hard.

Living the Days after in Dallas

"Mom." I heard Fury's voice but didn't instantly react. "Mom?" he gently repeated. "Did you forget to sign me up?"

With his name absent from the season finale Champs swim meet heat sheet, I didn't blame him for wondering. I'd forgotten before. But this time the omission wasn't my fault or the coach's.

On another day, the omission might have fired my ire—the inconvenience, the disappointment, and the unfairness of it all.

But not today.

Life's overwhelming events of late—with all their death, heartache, strife, and emotion—weighed heavier than a heat-sheet omission. Dallas had just endured the unimaginable.

On July 7, 2016, Micah Johnson ambushed and fired upon a group of police officers "at the end of a peaceful protest against nationwide officer-involved shootings"—killing five officers and injuring seven others, including two civilians.[1] Actions that, in and of themselves, ushered in overwhelming sadness and disbelief. But since the event occurred during a march, deep-seated and very hard to solve racial issues took center stage. The grief was palpable. The dynamics staggering. The issues unsolvable—at least at that moment. It was all too much.

With all that just on the other side of a school natatorium's doors, a heat-sheet omission seemed irrelevant. I was ready to chalk it up to a good life lesson (sometimes things don't work out despite our best-laid plans). I reached for my keys to go home, but before we made it to the door, the meet coordinator swooped in and took care of the oversight. He put Fury in the events for which he had been slotted.

So I took my place in the stands to watch.

Sort of.

How could we watch and cheer for swimming when a quarter of our downtown was a crime scene? How could we scream "Go!" when people were screaming hate at each other? And even closer to home, how could I be excited for the momentary when dear friends were suffering from the untimely deaths of loved ones, from relentlessly brutal sickness, job loss, spousal unfaithfulness, debilitating depression, suicide . . . and more?

Regular matters seemed so insignificant in light of those things.

But life goes on. Time marches, seconds tick, minutes pass, hours and days go by with little regard for the things that fill them—whether heavy or light.

Personally, I'd found it hard of late to get my productivity engine going in the midst of life's heavy moments. Like running in quicksand, we struggled to get beyond the heaviness.

But there we sat. At a swim meet in a sweltering hot, yet lovely, natatorium on a school's beautiful campus. In the moment, I might have even begrudged that school's first-world amenities, the parking lot filled with nice cars, the spectators in nice, clean clothes. When much of the rest of the world fights to find a bucket of clean water, these kids were swimming in it. Again, I felt nausea at the overwhelming nature of it all.

But as I watched, I noticed a few things that offered perspective on living in the midst of heavy moments:

Always, and regardless of events, people matter.

We saw it in downtown Dallas. I saw it play out from the stands.

After a confused start and a particularly dismal finish by our teen boys' relay team against a group of what looked more like college athletes, I watched them hop out of the water and head straight to shake hands. The trading of "great jobs" and "nice races" overshadowed the fair/not-fair event and made it about the people. I watched the boys on both sides appreciate each other.

It was compelling—even a little convicting.

Though tempted to believe otherwise, we're not alone.

If we look up, take note, and talk to the person walking alongside us, we may discover that they are feeling the same way we are.

"This is crazy," my friend Robin said. "I'm fighting feelings of frustration with the organization of this meet and so much more, which seems so petty and ridiculous, considering five people lost their lives yesterday. Perspective, huh?"

Yes. He said it; I needed to hear it. He outed the elephant in the room while fighting to find ground through perspective.

For me, my feelings weren't about swim-meet frustration but a nagging heaviness that was silently stealing the moment. His acknowledgment helped diffuse the covert threat. He outed the culprit, helped frame the moment, and most importantly, helped diffuse it by saying what we all were thinking—even if it was in the back of our minds.

Good is in the midst of bad.

Fred Rogers's reminder never gets old: "When I was a boy and I would see scary things in the news, my mother would say to me, 'Look for the helpers. You will always find people who are helping.'"[2] A great reminder to look up and see beyond.

People are resilient.

Resilience is part of the package, so lean into it.

We could all take a lesson from the cutest little six-year-old from a team in Frisco swimming the backstroke. His tiny body and determined windmill arms looked like a Happy Meal windup toy as he literally inched along the length of the pool, swimming his little heart out while everyone else finished. Head bobbing up and down as he gasped for air, he finally made it to the end of the pool amid the loud cheers of the crowd. Some kids might have cried, given up, or been embarrassed. He just got out and walked past the crowd unfazed, ready for the next event.

I think that's called grit. He inspired us all to keep going, regardless of the circumstances, to finish the race.

Moments matter.

It had been hard to allow moments to matter with life's heaviness loud and proud. But that meet mattered. The participants' hard work mattered. The races mattered. None of what took place was life defining, but it mattered. Regular life moments matter. And they might bring with them a richness of their own.

After watching Fury finish last in the event for which he had trained all summer, my heart sank as he walked my way.

"You okay?" I asked.

"I'm great," he responded. Then he added, "I know I came in last. But I shaved four seconds off my best time."

I was glad we had stayed.

It's good for life to go on.

Heavy life events happen and must be addressed (the hurt, the fear, the anxiety . . .), but we also need to respect the present. Life's heaviness, in the form of circumstances or stress or pressures, just can't be given any more reign than it already has. Maybe it's in life going on that life's heaviness doesn't win.

And these are only a few of the things that offered perspective.

May we let life's challenging circumstances, even heaviness, inform but never define our days, or our outlook. Rather than be overwhelmed by these moments, be overwhelmed by Truth.

Walking into that swim meet, Life's Overwhelmed tempted to steal so much. But Truth-reminders scattered throughout the natatorium on a very regular day flooded my eyes and mind.

And, maybe we can take a cue from the two US presidents who, despite their different backgrounds and ideologies, stood together at the Meyerson memorial service in Dallas that week, grieved, and purposed to inspire.

Then may we do as President George W. Bush encouraged: Reach for "the unity of hope, affection, and high purpose," avoid "judg[ing]

From History

Many will probably ask, Why do we have to wait? Why doesn't God straighten out things right now? The answer is found in the fact that God seems to work in strides. He doesn't do things all at once. Even the Genesis writer realized this. In his conception, God could have spoken and the whole universe would have come into being all at once, but instead he chose to spread it out over six days. Apparently God sees that his purpose in the universe can best be realized by working in strides. An all at once method of creation would not give man a chance to grow and develop. He would be a blind automaton. So God chooses to work in strides. This is why a theory of evolution should never frighten us. May it not be that God is working through the evolutionary process?

Wait, therefore, on the Lord. Your circumstance may seem to overwhelm you now, but wait on the Lord. Some disappointing experience may have you shivering in the cold winter of despair, but wait on the Lord.

Martin Luther King Jr.[3]

other groups by their worst examples, while judging ourselves by our best intentions, . . . practice empathy, imagining ourselves in the lives and circumstances of others. This is the bridge across our nation's deepest divisions—divisions that often overwhelm."[4]

This bridge is supported by the secret sauce of life: loving others—walking alongside rather than against. But how can we see if our eyes are locked in on only our circumstances or even anchored on ourselves? We might be surprised when we look up to find more than we expected.

Looking Up

Barton and I sat in the car at a red light waiting for green. I was going on hour two of carpool—not because we were traveling outside a five-mile radius of our house but because staggered school end times, plus drama practice, plus track practice resulted in lots of waiting. I don't mind. Especially if I'm sitting next to one of my six favorite people.

I looked out my window and saw a leafless tree.

"Boy, that tree looks sad, doesn't it?" I commented on one of three trees growing in the median green space.

"It looks dead," she replied.

But right next to it stood an almost exact replica—same height, same shape, and same type—but very different.

Spring had sprung on the second tree. Life hidden behind an outside that looked dead had made its way to the surface. That's what happens with spring. New life emerges. Whether seen with the human eye or hidden from sight, the life that springs forth from within is certain.

I love the way God often uses nature to remind us of so many of his eternal Truths. Barton and I talked about some of them.

Faith is being sure of what we hope for, certain of what isn't seen.[5] Faith informs situations in which what we see is the farthest thing from the whole picture. There's more to the story of those leafless trees—as there is in life.

Neither of us had to think hard to come up with something in our own journeys that felt lifeless. For her, an important friendship had gone south, a class always felt like an uphill battle, ever-present stress and pressures toyed with her and her friends and in a heartbeat could transport her back to the day she read the text about B.

We talked about timing. Certain things, people, situations might sprout and bloom before others. But that timing doesn't define a tree's worth or ours.

We talked about suffering and grief that can leave us feeling dead or damaged or worthless with nothing beautiful to show, but we can rest assured that there is more than meets the eye. Life comes from within—whether seen or unseen—from the roots planted in rich soil, especially by "streams of water."[6]

And then we talked about Easter—the greatest story of what looked dead actually conquering death to never die again. Enter hope stage left. Well, hope and peace and joy and life.

As we continued on, those trees lingered in my mind.

I was reminded of Steven Curtis Chapman's song "Spring Is Coming," written after the tragic death of their five-year-old daughter, Maria. That family lived the hardest of the hard. A son, a daughter, an accident, a tragic death—and momentarily dormant but hope-maintaining life that could barely be seen.

He recently joined us for a chat on *SaySomething Show*. He shared this nugget of Truth:

> We are all on a journey carrying grief and sadness and longing and ache in our heart for what isn't as it should be, for what is unfixable on this side of heaven. . . . And yet the hope that keeps us breathing and keeps us taking the next step is that the story is not over yet. . . . What it looks like, the way it appears right now, is not the end of the story. That's the gospel, that's the hope that we have.[7]

The hope that we have is the same yesterday, today, and forever. It's the hope that King David relied on when he found himself in a desperate spot, when he had nothing left to give. In that moment, he did what he had done since he had been a teenager tending sheep: he looked up. Then David shared in poetic song what he saw:

> I lift up my eyes to the mountains—
>   where does my help come from?
> My help comes from the LORD,
>   the Maker of heaven and earth.
> The LORD watches over you—
>   . . . both now and forevermore.[8]

Looking up takes our eyes from the situation or moment.

It's like Snopes when she "runs," ending her exercise routine with her favorite part—lying down in the middle of our neighboring park's field, looking up at the vastness of the sky, and allowing her mind to take in the enormity of the universe. Resting in the knowledge that the sun and the moon and stars come into and out of view every single day.

"I love it," she had told me. "It's so refreshing. My day melts into the bigger picture of life with the promise that a new day will dawn tomorrow. It's so peaceful and quiet and steady."

Maybe that's the beauty of looking up—eyes off us and onto something bigger, which can happen any time of the day.

"Hey! Look!" I punched my shotgun passenger, Barton. We were stuck in a long line of traffic, almost home, and absolutely tired of being in the car. "A rainbow!"

"Where?" she asked.

"It's right there." I pointed over the trees.

As we inched up the road, she moved her head, trying to see through the trees, not really believing me that there was a rainbow since it was not cloudy, let alone rainy.

Soon enough, we inched out from under the trees. "Can you see it now?"

Barton saw the breathtaking rainbow and stared. It was so beautiful. A tiny rainbow anchored in a barely noticeable rain cloud in the sunny sky. She snapped a picture and sent it to me.

Then we talked about God's promise—the story behind rainbows. How his faithfulness remains in every season and landscape—it's always there whether we see it or not. Not every rain cloud is obvious or apparent to others, yet God's promise stays true always. And I thought about my friends in dire straits who were suffering with health issues, about kids living in a day and age of perpetual pressures, about overwhelming societal and cultural issues that seem too big to handle, and how the Lord is faithful in the midst of life's heaviest circumstances.

Later I did what every techno-savvy gal does these days. I posted the picture on Instagram: "Don't forget to look up—you never know what you might see: a tiny rainbow on a sunny day."

Almost instantly, my friend Peggy replied, "And an angel wing." Isn't it nice that friends can help us see more than we do on our own? Sure enough, at the top of the rainbow, a wispy cloud perfectly resembled a wing—as if the Artist himself had skillfully painted it.

Maybe the tiny rainbow was a gentle reminder for me to keep my eyes focused up. I don't know. But I hope I remember to look up—on a sunny day as well as a stormy one.

Looking up might help the looking out too. The action peels our eyes away from distractions so we are able to see more in the moment. Remembering to look up can turn our focus away from life's craziness, and maybe even help slow things down a bit. And slowing down almost always brings with it a nice, long deep breath, and a little sanity—even in traffic.

> Worry doesn't empty tomorrow of its sorrows. It empties today of its strength.
>
> Corrie ten Boom[9]

Water Station

PRACTICING TRUST

Ginger Ravella, the widow of Air Force Major Troy Gilbert, posted the following on Facebook in honor of their twins' birthday. The picture wasn't quite what she expected it would be when the girls were born, six months before Troy was deployed to Iraq in 2006. Troy's F-16 was shot down while he was saving the lives of sixty fellow Americans. Upon impact, al Qaeda fighters raced in and stole Troy's body from the crash site as a trophy which traded hands for ten years until he was miraculously recovered in 2016 and buried a final time in Arlington Cemetery. Ginger's story is a terrific example of what it looks like to preach trust—today and every day.

> Today we celebrated Aspen & Annalise pictured here on their 12th birthday and 1st birthday.
>
> The 11 years in between these two photos are comprised of so much more than time or oohing and aahing over how much they've grown (though, my how they've grown! ;-)). I look back and see me and my Mom holding them as babies. That picture doesn't capture the whole story. My smile hid the sorrow in my heart. Of all the birthdays that should be celebrated with both [parents], it should be the first one. Their Dad had just died. He wasn't there and honestly, because he wasn't, I wasn't either . . .
>
> And tonight, on their 12th birthday, they giggled with friends and smiled big brace-face smiles and blew out candles just like I always imagined they would when I gazed upon their tiny new-born faces. They love and laugh and hope and dream. They have friends and family and wholeness just like I prayed for.
>
> On their first birthday, I couldn't see how God could do any of that. How would He ever finish their stories with happy endings? I don't know how He did it, but I guess that's not really any of my business. That's what makes Him so marvelously mysterious. At the end of this week's episode of "This Is Us" in between bouts of ugly crying, I was shocked to see the previews for next week's show?! I guess I honestly thought the show ended because Jack

died. Or that there wasn't anything left to say. But I was wrong. Both about the tv show and about our future. There were more chapters to be written, not just in the twins' lives but in our family's story. . . .

Life isn't television. You don't get to sneak a peek at the previews. Not knowing what's ahead is probably for our own good. The terrifying twists would paralyze us, keeping us from fully living in the present. The terrific turns would fixate us on the future, missing the growth that happens in the waiting. Not knowing enables us to fully wrap our arms around truly trusting our Father.

If you're reading this and wondering how you'll live through something or what will happen in the next episode of your life, rest in the fact that you don't have to have it figured out. God does. The memories of who you were will be woven into the fabric of who you will become. Not that I still don't cry a little with each kids' birthday . . . I'm human and being human means we still hurt. It's ok to have hard days, even to have birthdays that are more empty than they are full. The God of the Universe is never too big or too busy to be about you and your dreams.

Ten

Rather Than Be Overwhelmed by Bitterness, Be Overwhelmed by Forgiveness

> Problems cannot be solved at the same level of consciousness that
> created them.
>
> Albert Einstein

"Have you ever been depressed?" my friend Dana asked. I had just come in from Wichita Falls where I had attended my uncle's funeral and picked her up to go to a visitation for a friend's husband. My uncle had lived a long, fruitful life, dying at a ripe old age. Not so for this man. Depression and other health issues had played a role.

"Not really. Not in the way you're asking, I don't think," I answered. "I did experience postpartum depression with one of the kids—of course, it was before people openly talked about it. It was so odd. I was incredibly anxious and cried all the time. I had no idea what was wrong with me. And I was so afraid it was my new normal—until it went away after a few weeks." I returned the question. "Have you?"

"I have," she replied and went on to tell me about an experience that had left her a little off. Much of it stemmed from a work experience with people she trusted who trampled upon that trust. I think the fact that they were people of faith made it all the worse, leaving her in a funk. But, she didn't run or hide from the situation; she did her best to figure out why deep sadness had settled in, which led her back to broken relationships, being wronged, and feelings of bitterness. Her bitterness.

And she told me she realized that in order to move on, she needed to deal with harbored feelings that had hidden themselves in justifiable bitterness. In the hope of finding peace, she found herself compelled to go and apologize for the bitterness she had felt towards the people involved. Dana certainly wasn't giving an okay to what had been done. And she wasn't asking for an apology from anyone. She simply wanted to be done with the continued hurt and negative feelings she couldn't shake after all that had happened.

Prudently, Dana sought wise counsel before doing something that seemed counter to all she would think to be true. After which she met with a few of the people involved and confessed her bitterness. I love that she didn't hide the issue or run and isolate herself—which we so often do when hurt or shamed. And that she allowed herself to be known—something that is hard to do with trust involved—as in "Can I trust the person on the other side?" Dana hoped that she could. But regardless, people she could trust were traveling alongside her. Through the process, Dana's bitterness was literally uprooted. Surprisingly, at least to her, forgiveness bloomed in its place.

The world questions how forgiving or apologizing to someone who has hurt us could ever be beneficial. But bitterness rarely hurts the offender, only the one holding on to it. Here's where counterintuitive wisdom comes in and brings freedom with it.

Dana basically said no to bitterness, relinquished the world-given right to feel that way (she had absolutely been wronged), and did what seemed ludicrous. On the other side, the peace and the freedom she experienced surprised and even floored her. So much so that she felt compelled to look back on her life to see if she was harboring bitterness for any other events that might have hurt.

As I listened to the freedom from deep relational hurt that she was experiencing, I wanted it too. I went home that night and asked God to show me if I was harboring bitterness toward anyone. And sure enough, clear as day, I realized there were a few on that list—people who had desperately hurt me and someone I love. And they had done it with their eyes open, justifying their actions—likely still considering the actions to be right.

For years, I've struggled with anger related to these people and the situation. I was faced with it often, since I was continually in the environment where it had occurred. But until I contemplated bitterness and called it out, I had never actually considered the fact that bitterness was at play, hurting me, keeping me a prisoner to the situation.

So after talking with safe friends, I decided to follow Dana's example and confess my bitterness to one of the parties involved. I knew it would be awkward for both of us, but I needed to let my bitterness go. So I stepped forward with a bumbling apology along these lines:

> This is going to sound weird, so thank you for listening. I've never done this before, but here goes. I need to apologize to you. I've been harboring bitterness and a little anger toward you for what happened years ago, what was done to X and to our family. I'd like to apologize to you for that. I'm sorry. I know this is strange, but I think I need to apologize for my bitterness in order to let go of it. I don't need anything from you. In fact, I genuinely don't want anything. I just need to admit my part and move on. I don't think

you intended to hurt us. In fact, I think you probably did what you thought was right, but those actions significantly injured us.

She accepted my apology. She was probably the only one in the scenario who would have received my bumbling attempt, which I knew before going in. And she told me, "I would never intentionally hurt someone, let alone X or you." Which I knew to be true. But her actions still hurt.

She let it sink in. Then asked, "Is X okay?"

In the craziest way, with my heart already lighter, I could answer her without bitterness or resentment. "No, X is not. But I trust God who redeems even wounded souls." Because I do.

I did my best to do the same with others involved in that bitterness, only not to their face. It wouldn't have been prudent; so instead I wrote a letter but didn't send it. I even went so far as to read the letter to one of my friends who helped me process. Somehow that allowed the hurts to be said out loud and received.

I have a friend who did the same thing with her father even though he had died years earlier. She took a friend with her and read a letter she had written to him—calling out things he had done to her. She found significant healing and freedom from things that had stolen life for years. Wounds are a part of every life—why not put one foot in front of the other in an effort to help healing occur and refuse to allow the enormity and the overwhelming nature of heart hurt to steal joy from today?

Which is exactly what bitterness does—it steals from today. What a reminder to keep roots of bitterness shallow and accounts short. To instead be overwhelmed by forgiveness—both the granted and received—and surprised by freedom even in issues of the heart that seem almost untouchable. Like most of our other efforts to reframe Life's Overwhelmed, the fix isn't easy or instant, but the steps are on solid ground. The process of taking the steps might seem precarious and filled with uncertainty. Even those steps are lined with mysterious

Psychology Today blogger Stephen Diamond defines bitterness as "a chronic and pervasive state of smoldering resentment . . . one of the most destructive and toxic of human emotions."

Psychologist and author Leon Seltzer asserts that the cure for bitterness is forgiveness: "Forgiveness alone enables you to let go of grievances, grudges, rancor and resentment. . . . It can hardly be over-emphasized that when you decide to forgive your perceived wrong-doer, you're doing so not so much for them but for yourself." And, drawing on James Messina, he proposes steps for moving beyond your resentment:

- "Identify the source of your bitterness and what this person did to evoke your resentful feelings."
- "Develop a new way of looking at your past, present, and future—including how resentment has negatively affected your life and how letting go of it can improve your future."
- "Write a letter to this person, describing [their] offenses toward you, then forgive and let go of them (but don't send the letter)."[1]

beauty as people travel alongside us and as our need to be known is met at deep spiritual levels when we call out and let go of hurt.

Maybe in allowing ourselves to be open and honest, we give people next to us the same freedom.

Short Accounts

"I have to tell you that you hurt my feelings," Birdie said to me on his way to shower.

Those were zinger words. I instantly wanted to justify whatever I had said in order to somehow make those words go away, to make them not my fault. But I've learned through the years that it's better to meet hard things head-on rather than stuff them down, only to revisit them in later years when they have deeper roots.

"I'm sorry," I began, genuinely remorseful—but how far can sorry go without knowing or owning its basis? "I think I can guess what I did, but would you rather tell me?"

He didn't hesitate. "You embarrassed me in front of my friend when you asked about my project."

I was thankful he felt safe enough to say what I had done. And he was right. I had done that.

Safe is important. But can be hard to remember when faced with hurtful words. Recently Boxster redirected my thoughts when the words of a lifelong and very close friend had hurt me and continued to sting. My gut reaction was to shut down, grab hold of temptations to ignore, and to quit. But here's where honesty, walking alongside, and being willing to beat Life's Overwhelmed at its own game come into play.

As we made our way through the drive-through at Chick-fil-A, Boxster asked what was bothering me, so I told him. We're pretty honest in our home. I don't want to hide things from my kids—especially as they get older.

His response overwhelmed me. "She's one of your best friends. You know, those are the only people who are willing to be completely honest with us. Everyone else acts all nice, pretends to care, but walks away and talks about you behind your back. You should be glad she told you what she thought. It shows she cares."

Preach it.

He was right. He stopped my pity party right there. He helped me be able to put aside words that felt rude and hurtful and label them correctly as a friend being a friend—not a fake—out of love. Because Boxster was next to me and listened, he could do what I couldn't—see beyond the pain and offer perspective and Truth.

I was put in my place right there on the spot in the Chick-fil-A drive-through. Rather than wallowing, overwhelming gratitude replaced the hurt—not only for a good and long-standing friendship but for nice and honest people traveling alongside me—namely my kids.

Which is where I found myself when facing Birdie's honesty that I had hurt his feelings. Earlier in the afternoon, he and his friend had come in from running around the neighborhood. They were sweaty and happy and ready to play Just Dance on the Wii. As I looked at the two sitting next to each other on the couch, I couldn't stop myself. After tossing out a few how's-your-week-going pleasantries, I asked his friend, "Have you done your project?"

"Oh yeah," he said. "I finished that a while ago." Then he asked Birdie, "Have you finished? Which option did you like better?"

Birdie simply rolled with it. "I haven't done it all, so it's kind of hard to say."

For weeks, I had been having the conversation I seem to have from time to time when something like a project or assignment enters our world. It's a broken-record chat in which I say, "Have you started your project?" Which is a manipulative question because we both know the answer. *No.* But somehow I feel it is my duty to check and point out. Shame always seems to be on the other side of such checks.

Oh, the fine line of accountability.

Having instantly regretted my question, since it put someone I love in an awkward spot, I quickly changed the subject. Old me would have outed the kid in front of his friend in some feigned attempt to make the other person feel good about their accomplishment. But I stopped short, thankfully.

Clearly, I had overstepped my boundary by asking his friend. And deep down, I knew I had. So as I stood and faced a person whose feelings I had hurt, I tried to own up to what I had done.

"I really am sorry. At best I had hoped he'd inspire you to finish. I didn't mean to embarrass you. Clearly I did. And I'm sorry—again."

Overwhelmed had silently slipped into our house over the last few weeks, the door having been opened by change. Of our five kids, three were facing significant changes in their landscape. I guess with all the unknowns and uncertainties, I just wanted a few loops closed, like a project finished before its due date, since the capacity I had to handle curveballs was getting smaller and smaller by the day.

Overwhelmed loves to ride on the coattails of things like change—especially change that can evoke old memories or emotions we might not have realized carry stress. We bring to the table all the history of past events that inform today.

There was probably a lot more under-the-surface action going on for me. Likely fear. And fear often brings with it my knee-jerk reaction to control. The thing about fear is that it tricks us into thinking we know what's going to happen. Granted there are logical processions, but fears are often unfounded.

Overwhelmed invites self-doubt and uncertainty along for fun. Then it sprinkles "I can't" like fertilizer on a dormant lawn and sits back to watch the weeds germinate. But they're just weeds—they're a nuisance and they need pulling. They can grow only so high and are actually easily seen when they surface. That's right where Overwhelmed can be turned to good. Countless issues lie dormant until we see them, though they often stay hidden until we're overwhelmed by them.

With Birdie's project, I am thankful for an honest kid who keeps short accounts—meaning they are dealt with now rather than shelved for a later day. The funk surfaced quickly. I needed to own my part, so I tried. "I'm sorry I called you out in front of a friend. It was wrong. I didn't mean to"—but did I? Probably.

I likely did it because I love that kid.

I don't want the year to start off with a red mark.

Red marks bring up old feelings that I hate, usually associated with hurt, hurt from another one of our kids' struggles during the same grade. Words like *brutal*, *heartbreaking*, *cruel*, and so many more came to mind as descriptors. It was a little scary to be staring at those waters again. That's where Life's Overwhelmed can enter the picture—ready to ignite embers of past pain. But here's where we say no. None of this is the boss of us. Instead bring on

The Power of Extending Forgiveness

Eva Kor was ten years old when she entered Auschwitz in 1944 with her identical twin sister, Miriam. After enduring the journey from Romania to the death camp (seventy hours in an overstuffed train car without food or water), she and her sister were separated from their mother, father, and siblings, never to see them again.

The Germans, always on the lookout for twins, instantly informed Dr. Mengele of their arrival. Whisked to his barracks, the girls took their place as human guinea pigs. Inhumane experiments were conducted on each pair of twins collected off the trains.

Every day blood was drawn from the Kor girls, after which Eva would receive five injections, the contents of which she was never able to identify. Months into the ordeal, an injection made her deathly ill. According to Eva, Mengele himself came to her when she was so sick. He took one look, turned to the other doctors, and sarcastically said, "Too bad. She's so young. She has only two weeks to live." But she defied him and lived, surviving the horrific ordeal and many after until the day she and her sister were famously photographed at the front of the line when the death camp was liberated on January 27, 1945.

Fifty years after the liberation of Auschwitz, Eva returned to the site and stood where so many had

some forgiveness—of ourselves and of others—see the future as fresh, not a victim of the past, and start to be overwhelmed by the freedom that comes with it.

States of Matter—People

This morning I woke with a heavy heart for one of my suffering friends. It's a struggle to know where to put all the emotion that comes with suffering and sickness.

Because it's all there.

been tragically murdered. At her side was Dr. Hans Münch, a Nazi doctor who had known Dr. Mengele but had not worked with him. Eva read Dr. Münch's signed witness statement to contradict those who denied the Holocaust. To the surprise of many, she then freed herself from her victim status. In her name only, she forgave Dr. Mengele and the Nazis. An incredible weight of suffering was lifted, and she felt strong. Though it did not mean she would forget what had happened, offering forgiveness healed Eva.

> What I discovered for myself was life-changing. I discovered that I had the power to forgive. No one could give me that power and no one could take it away. It was all mine to use in any way I wished . . .

I imagined Mengele was in the room with me. I picked up a dictionary and wrote down 20 nasty words which I read clear and loud to that make-believe Mengele in the room. And at the end I said, "In spite of all that, I forgive you. . . ." [It] made me feel good. I, the guinea pig of 50 years, even had the power over the Angel of Death of Auschwitz.

I felt free. Free from Auschwitz. Free from Mengele. But now that I had forgiven him, I knew that most of the survivors denounced me, denounce me today. But what is my forgiveness? I like it. It is an act of self-healing, self-liberation, self-empowerment. . . .

I want people to remember that we can never change what happened. That is the tragic part. But we can change how we relate to it.[2]

The fear. The anxieties. The not-fairs. The pain. The questions, mostly centered on why and how. How could something so bad happen to such a wonderful person? Why is it someone so young with a young child and loving husband? Why such high levels of pain? Why months, likely days, left instead of years? So we travel the road together.

The last few weeks had made me so grateful for the way these friends have lived their lives. And it hit home yet again the importance of being hydrated *before* hitting any incline of life's mountains.

Not every day, but this day I was sad. Two very dear friends. Two terminal diagnoses. Two plates filled with pain.

The tears sat perched, threatening to rain, so I decided to head to the pool for a swim, as my gym pal Florence says, "to get the poison out."

Since my mind was so filled with heavy thoughts, I forgot to bring a towel. Most fitness centers provide towels, but at ours, there is a new rule—a one-towel rule. Apparently, patrons must have been using too many of the center's towels. Being that the towels are about the size of a postage stamp, I understand why! In response to the towel overuse, the powers that be had clamped down and put forth a one-towel-per-patron rule.

Realizing I had forgotten my towel and knowing that I had to shower after my swim, I decided to ask the check-in gal if I could just this once have an extra towel. I didn't think it would be too big of an ask since two postage-stamp-size towels actually equal one standard-size towel.

After check-in gal happily sent the elderly lady in front of me on her way, she turned to me.

"What can I do for you?"

"Well," I said, handing her my membership card to be swiped, "I don't need a locker, but I do need a towel."

Dressed in a pirate outfit for Halloween, she took my card, eyed me a bit, and handed me a towel off the top of her stack.

"And," I ventured sheepishly, feeling a bit like George Costanza standing in front of the Soup Nazi, aware that her fun holiday attire only masked a rigid rule follower, "is there any way I could have an extra towel?"

Her smile instantly faded to ice.

So I nervously stammered, "I forgot mine. I never do, but I forgot it today."

A chilly smile returned as she chirped, "Absolutely not. There is only one towel per member." She cocked her head, raised her eyebrow for good measure, then addressed the man coming in the door behind me with a syrupy, "Well, hello!"

I tried once more.

"I really always bring my own towel, but—"

"I said *one* towel only," she low-growled, followed by a sugary, "Locker 52, Mr. Anderson?"

Her words landed like a solid punch to my already upset stomach.

I took the tiny towel and wondered how in the world I would be able to swim, shower, and dry off with a rag.

As I made my way to the pool, I wanted to run back and yell at her, "Give me an extra towel, lady! You have no idea what is going on in my life. I just need a towel. Check my account. I'm not a habitual towel forgetter. Just this once please be nice to me. I need nice. My friends are dying!"

I cried while I swam, stopping periodically at the end of a lap to empty my goggles of tears. As I waged war with my thoughts, I was moved to consider how something as silly as someone's unnecessary rudeness could overwhelm my already filled-to-full thoughts.

I decided to use this opportunity to practice dealing with unnecessary rudeness—an issue that hits us as we travel this busy life. It comes in the form of honking our horns, stealing parking spaces, and cutting in line. It comes from curt salespeople, grumpy customers, stressed parents, overworked colleagues, and exhausted kids whose fuses are short. And if we forget to notice one small detail in the equation, we might be tempted to let it get the best of us with words we don't mean to say slipping right out of our mouths.

The detail: people.

I wanted to yell at the towel police, "I'm a person! Just a person. And there's more going on inside than what you see on the outside."

But as my laps built one upon the other, my thoughts made headway too. Because I know better. And I've learned that even on life's hard roads, we can be overwhelmed by good. And steps,

179

or strokes in this case, toward freedom usually begin in the same place—consideration of the people around us.

The towel gal is a person.

She's a person just like me. Who knows how many people have griped at her over the new rule? She might have bristled, readying herself for backlash, expecting me to blast her like countless others. She's a person. A person doing her job.

Then I thought about the towel. Beyond its small size, the one she had handed me was especially rough, like sandpaper, which at first made me even more frustrated. I wanted to march back and say, "If I get only one, at least let it be a soft towel," until I started to think about the person behind me. Who knows what's going on in his life? Maybe he needs a soft one more than I do.

With my thoughts adjusting and the sting of what had felt like a slap fading—I actually started to breathe. I didn't want to be overwhelmed by budding bitterness, justified anger, or to allow grief to overstep and overinform an exchange that, on any other day, would have been a blip. And I urged myself to remember that in every situation, especially those laced with what can feel like an attack, such as unnecessary rudeness, there are people, just people, on the other side. People who are likely dealing with tough situations. So regardless of what they hand me, I want to do my best to return with a smile or a gentle response.

Gentle responses, forgiveness, and the powerful tool of considering others soothes the souls of all involved.

Water Station

CLUTTER CONTROL—AN INSTANT BOOST
WHEN LIFE FEELS OVERWHELMING

In our world, clutter looks a little something like this. We walk in the door from wherever and set our stuff on the counter. With seven bodies in our home, that can be lots of stuff. We take care of most of it. But little junky things that may or may not be worth keeping stay on the counter. Then we "clean up" but don't know quite what to do with the knickknacks.

So, we slide them into a drawer. No worries. It's only a few things and I can still grab the napkins so neatly stacked in my clean drawer. It works for a while.

Sure, I feel a teensy bit bad messing up my lovely napkin drawer, but each time I justify sliding leftover knickknacks into it by telling myself I'll deal with it tomorrow when I have time. But before I know it, I can't even find a napkin because the drawer is home to so many other things. So I convince myself that napkins should never have been in the drawer to begin with. It should have had junk status to begin with.

Recently, while digging through the mess to find a pencil for Birdie, I couldn't help but think of how we have junk drawers in life. Like relationship issues that are conveniently put aside until another day. Because in the moment, the issue might not be that big of a deal. We can deal with it tomorrow. It doesn't matter. Until the tomorrows build up and all the minors have morphed into majors and we can't get to the bottom of the drawer due to well-intentioned avoidance.

It's not just relationships. All I have to do is look at my email inbox to see very real things that need attention. Most of the reasons that warranted my deal-with-it-tomorrow approach were reasonable. I just didn't know exactly what to do, or the issue wasn't dire, so tomorrow seemed fine.

How many and how long I put things off is probably the bigger issue. I never minded a few things in that drawer. But as we conveniently shoved stuff inside, I didn't realize how full it had become and how hard it would be to find what I needed since we could barely pry it open.

Keeping accounts short and keeping the clutter at a minimum sure can alleviate stress. Especially as years march on and we open all the life-drawers that may have been overstuffed for a while.

Because the truth is, we feel better—physically, emotionally, and spiritually—with the drawers less cluttered. The nicest part: no one is asking for complete clean *and* it's not a road you have to go alone.

So any time life begins to weigh in and weigh down, quickly gut check with wash, rinse, repeat, then take practical steps to lighten the load like, but certainly not limited to:

- Declutter the car console while waiting in the carpool line.
- Pick a drawer, any drawer, and de-junkify.
- Take a sack up to any closet, walk in with it empty and out with it full. Then take it directly to the car for drop-off donation that day.
- Take a box to any room—especially an office, kid's room, or living room—that might be holding on to old video cassettes and the like, fill it, and then add the contents to a donation run.
- For soul clutter, make a phone call to just say hi, connect, and start to pave the path toward peace.

"Why don't we just clean out the drawer?" Birdie asked, taking over the search for a pencil. And I thought, *Why not clean it out today? Sounds good to me.*

Of course, he added, "Will you pay me to help?" I laughed, grateful all the same to have someone to rummage through the junk with me.

I was even happier when Barton walked up with an offer to help. "We don't need that. Keep those. What in the world? For sure get rid of that."

The simple, yet slightly time-consuming, act of decluttering spaces in our home, drawers at work, or even a center console while waiting in the carpool line not only makes us physically feel better but quickly lightens the stress load that tempts us to think the amount of clutter only has one way to go—*up*.

Sometimes the simplest acts can momentarily put the kibosh on Overwhelmed—from performance pressures to identifier stress to choice anxiety to bitterness. Clearing out physical clutter provides a reprieve, gets our eyes off the moment, and jump-starts our effort to clear pressure and stress-laden clutter from our minds.

eleven

Rather Than Be Overwhelmed by Present Sufferings, Be Overwhelmed by an Eternal Perspective

Heaven is under our feet as well as over our heads.

Henry David Thoreau

On a recent drive down Florida's I-95, I turned to Barton, who was shotgun, and said, "It seems kind of boring and ugly and sort of claustrophobic, doesn't it?" Relentlessly guarded by a wall of trees, the road left a lot to the imagination.

"All of the above," she replied, straining to see the beautiful sunset we had admired only moments before getting on the highway. "I can't see the marsh anymore either."

We were traveling from Savannah to catch a flight home to Dallas via Jacksonville. The towering tree line came with obstructed-view seating. All the colors, the birds, and the beauty of the marsh grasses emerging from their soggy foundation could only be barely glimpsed, every so often, through gaps in the towering line of trees.

"It's funny, isn't it," I thought out loud, "that whether we can see the marsh or not has no bearing on its existence? All the beauty we were just admiring—the sun setting, the light shimmering on the barely noticeable water at the base of all the multicolored Southern Georgia marsh grasses—is still there."

My mind quickly moved from the trees and the marsh to life's suffering that acts like those trees filling our line of sight with towering gridlock and the promises that can be hard to see when an obstructed view informs the moment. We had crossed the six-month mark of H's death. Since then, the husband of one of my dearest friends had chosen the same route—which was almost too much to bear and absolutely too hard to believe. The hows and the whys seemed to be beating down our door as well as the doors of people we know and love.

"It makes me think of the suffering so many people we know have endured or are enduring," I continued, thinking about the terminal diagnoses of my friends Jen and Greg too. And about even closer to home, as in *within* our home, extreme heart hurt. "Suffering—so many things in life, really—can take over and make it easy to forget what's on the other side. But," I added, "in the same way those trees, though obstructing the view, have no bearing on the existence or the power of the beautiful setting sun—remember, the sun is there whether we can see it or not. Suffering, hardships, stresses, and pressures, though obstructing our view, have no effect on the existence or the power of the Son, who has defeated them all."

My thoughts turned to Jen.

She was diagnosed with cancer shortly after giving birth to her son, Lincoln—a sweet surprise to her and her newlywed husband, Scott. Surgeries, chemo, radiation, and therapies—all went to battle for Jen's life. Until the word *remission* replaced painful appointments on her calendar. But three years later, she was admitted to Baylor Hospital, where she was told that the cancer was back, and the prognosis wasn't good. The pain of a broken rib due to the ugly disease was being managed while they figured out what was next. They were hurting—physically and emotionally.

But Jen, with her heart breaking, stood firm—not on her own foundation but on God who never wavers, whose provision is always sufficient, even when circumstances beg us to fear otherwise. As she struggled to put one foot in front of the other—because she would press on as she always had—she stood strong in her faith, joyful, truly joyful, while crying at the same time.

A few months after Jen's cancer returned, when the members of our neighborhood Bible study were tossing around ideas for the summer, Jen floated an idea she had.

What would you all think about a summer study on heaven? Dare I dream we all set our sights on glory together?

The question, texted to our group of friends, probably caused a few hearts to skip a beat. It certainly caused mine to pause.

Of course the answer would be yes—for so many reasons. But be that as it may, just on the other side of those yeses stood a chorus of nos. No, we were not ready to admit that heaven's gates were getting close to welcoming the sender of the text.

The group replied back, fighting the tears, wrangling conflicted thoughts.

Absolutely.

The unexpected road on which we found ourselves was about to get all the more real. Though a road inevitably traveled by all, it's not one eagerly traveled by anyone. Death was standing on our friend's doorstep, ringing the bell. But the thing about death is that, though he sometimes announces his arrival, he doesn't need an invitation to come in.

There is something that causes a person whose days have been audibly numbered, and those walking alongside, to live today differently in light of tomorrow—the eternal tomorrow.

Jen had her eyes firmly set on the promise to come rather than allowing the suffering at hand to shape her outlook on the world. And she wanted us to look too. Hundreds joined us as we did. We aired the *ifs*, then encouraged each other and honed our focus to see the *thens*. Because, as Jen often said, all our days are numbered; her number had simply received an educated guess by a doctor.

So—

If hope is real, *then* we can land there rather than in a place of fear.

If people are what matter (as the saying goes, "Two things last forever: the Word of God and the souls of men"), *then* allow that Truth to inform our relationships here. Seeing and treating people with respect and dignity because they/we matter.

If sin is not a part of heaven, *then* allow its grip to be loosened here. This means breaking free from jealousy or self-absorption or shame or regret or trying to find our identity and self-worth in anything other than how God has defined it.

If in heaven we will be filled with joy and eternal pleasures,[1] *then* allow today's small joys and pleasures to teach us about the lasting ones to come. Any goodness in this life is a glimpse of the good and glory to come. Any suffering and sadness is a reminder that we aren't home yet.

If heaven is all about God, *then* allow that knowledge to help us find freedom from ourselves. "On this earth we make life all about grief, guilt, pain—we make it about ourselves," Jen said. "In this life we *should* all over ourselves and others—allowing pressures to control the volume. If we won't do it

Your life on earth is a dot. From that dot extends a line that goes on for all eternity. Right now you're living in the dot. But what are you living for? Are you living for the dot or for the line? Are you living for earth or for heaven? Are you living for the short today or the long tomorrow?

Randy Alcorn[2]

in God's presence—since *should, would,* and *could* won't exist—why give them so much power now?"

If in heaven all tears are wiped away (not some but all), *then* we can find hope today. Tomorrow's no more death, no more mourning, no more crying, no more pain can help ease the pain of all those things that still plague our Today.

Back on the highway to Jacksonville, I wondered if Jen's invitation to contemplate heaven offered part of the answer to navigating suffering, to seeing beyond the trees that can obstruct our view. Hers was an informed perspective. A perspective in light of eternity. A perspective that can help us live, not just exist, even when life is hard, any kind of hard. Because, like the marsh and the beautiful sunset hidden by the tall trees, more-than-meets-the-eye owns more real estate than life's difficulties could ever claim. It's the cornerstone of Faith.

"Whether my months have been numbered or not, I want to live more detached from this world and with more hope for the next," Jen said. Then she—always the teacher, the encourager, the contemplator of things to come—added an analogy:

Life is like a hotel room. I've never gone to a hotel room and tried to rearrange the furniture, hang pictures, take things out, and put things in. We don't think, *Oh, I'm going to live here for a week and make it awesome. I'm going to make this hotel room my home for a week.* I've never tried to make that my

188

home. That has never crossed my mind—because it is not my home. It is a hotel room, and I am literally passing through.

This image is so true for this life. This world is not our home—if we are in Christ. And yet we are planting such deep roots and we are rearranging and working and striving so hard to make this the place for life and joy and all things right as if this were our home. But in the same way we do not settle into a hotel room, we need to stay anchored in the truth that we are simply passing through. This world is not our home.

Now that's something worth meditating on.

Way too early for us, Jen did go home. Now not only is she seeing the other side of the trees but she is also living in all its joy and peace and splendor. And for those left behind, we experience a relationship interruption—a seemingly long road on this side of the trees. But it's a road paved with hope that promises immeasurably more than we could ever imagine.

Suffering and Joy

It seems we could all use a nice jolt of joy every once in a while. *Joy* is such an interesting word. It alludes to a concept more deeply rooted than happiness. In fact, *happiness* is often used to describe joy—as are *delight* and *bliss*. Joy originates from the Latin word *gaudēre*, "to rejoice."[3]

It can be hard to find joy today, especially amid the turmoil, sadness, information overload, and anger filling the airwaves. Well-intentioned people fight against each other for the last word, even on things like how to love well. Because how can love look to some like opening borders and to others like closing borders, among so many other heated topics.

Joy is the best make-up.
Ann Lamott[4]

189

I don't know, but it does. And so the concept of love gets brutalized in the crosshairs of a right way, and casualties grow as relationships crumble. We live in a strange world where conversations occur more online than they do in person, making it easy for people to say just about anything, no matter how scathing or hateful, sometimes forgetting the people on the other side of the conversation.

And we search to make sense of life. But where's the joy? Can we find joy, real joy, in the midst of social turmoil, atrocities, suffering, and heartache so that we can sing with honest hearts and true goodwill toward those traveling alongside us?

I remember sitting at our kitchen table with my father-in-law not so long ago, chatting about the topic of joy. He was in Dallas for a visit, a small breather from his own less-than-ideal life landscape at the time. His wife of fifty years had been taken prisoner by Alzheimer's. And due to the debilitating disease, literally everything in their life had changed. The dreams, the home, the occupation—all of it had been disrupted. Dick's new normal took him on a detour for roughly ten years—a road that wasn't sunshine and butterflies.

But he met the situation head-on, determined, searching for the meaning of joy in the midst of far less than cheerful circumstances.

How did he do it? In a manner that's worth contemplating as we travel our own road.

He grappled with joy—honestly, not in some Pollyanna way or in an effort to prove a point. He asked the question, What does it mean to "count it all joy"? And he asked with an open mind, keeping his own answers and desires at bay. I think that's why hope always met him in the midst.

He made the most of his situation, even though it was clearly a tough one. He was quick to take the focus off himself by constantly reaching out to those around him. In the ten or so years that he made a daily trek to an Alzheimer's unit, he was around lots of folks who needed an ear to hear their story or a good word to brighten their day. So he listened and encouraged.

He kept going. He didn't know the answer to counting it all joy, but determinedly—anchored in trust and hope—he put one foot in front of the other every day.

And, he fought to not fell prey to a victim mentality.

I've witnessed friends who were at the epicenter of suffering find joy the same way. At the height of her illness, Jen gently told my daughter who was struggling with what was happening to someone she loved, "People say to me, 'Do you ever ask why you?' to which I can honestly answer, 'No.' My question would be more along the lines of 'Why not me?' I feel bad for the people that don't get to walk the road I'm walking because they don't get to see God the way I do."

And then she added, "I need you to know that I'm not scared. I'm not scared of dying." She almost reached out to hold Snopes's face like you would a little child when you want them to listen. "It's not like I'm not scared at all—because I am scared of the pain. But I am not afraid of death. I can't wait to see and touch Jesus—even though I'm sad at the thought of leaving people I love and not getting to be with Lincoln as he grows up."

Powerful.

The why-not-me part is hard to imagine, but I've heard that same sentiment from others who are facing hard times in life. My brother's friend Kyle Ogle is among them. Kyle's cancer diagnosis and treacherous road included an arm amputation in his midtwenties—devastating for anyone but especially for someone who loved all things sport, including hunting. But he rarely let anything slow him down. He made a special attachment for his bow so he could hold the arrow and string in his teeth. In 2005, he was named Pagosa Country Adventure Guide's "Hunter of the Year."

Here is something he shared in the midst of his battle:

191

We will continue to follow this treatment routine as long as our doctor feels it is safe. Eventually we will have to find a new game, but for now this is where we are. This is our "normal." We will be busy with work, school, etc. with our favorite added bonuses of Katherine's soccer games and Turner's baseball games. We love this time of year.

I gave my life to Jesus and asked him to save me from sin when I was seventeen. My life has not turned out exactly as I thought it would. It does not say next to my picture in our high school yearbook "Most Likely to Get Cancer at twenty-six and Win the One-Armed Dove Hunt." It would be an understatement to say that life has been difficult the last few years. God never promised me an easy life or great wealth, just an abundant life.

Things have been excruciatingly hard at times, but we have lived. It hasn't been the kind of every day monotonous do it all again the next day kind of living. We have experienced more love, more joy, more kindness, and more miracles than most people see in one hundred years of living. That is abundance. I have a lot of games to attend, so I hope that abundant life continues for years to come.

But the greatest promise he gave was that when this life is over, there is more to come. Out with the abundant life and in with the eternal. The story will not end here. In fact, it will not end, ever.

Joy is in the midst.

Anchored in hope.

And in the midst of my father-in-law's journey—along the entirety of its way—joy paved his path, even and especially, when happiness took a backseat to tears.

Maybe some seeing beyond the moment—practicing joy today anchored in hope—can make the words mean a little more than they might have in the past. Surely practicing joy today can help us see above the world's chaos and spot pockets of peace—and then to see beyond ourselves. Because it's likely that someone will cross our paths today who needs to be heard or seen.

Heaven Glimpses Today

As can probably be imagined, with five kids in the house we've seen our fair share of the dentist's office. Maybe I am getting older because a lot of those trips have been for me. One trip was to our periodontist. He checked my teeth, then my bite, and asked, "Are you under any stress?"

I thought for a minute, mentally filing through areas in my life, then replied, "Nope. I can't think of anything." I really couldn't.

"How many kids do you have?" he asked, more like reminded.

"Five."

He looked at me, then at his assistant with an is-she-for-real look and said, "Let me assure you that with five kids you are absolutely under stress."

He wasn't kidding.

But neither was I. I honestly didn't think I had stress. Apparently the way I was grinding my teeth proved otherwise. So he prescribed, and took molds for, a mouth guard to be worn at night and "during carpool." Hilarious.

Not long ago I returned with a tooth gone bad and we got to talking. Since that's what I do—talk. Because, not only am I a founding member of the Women's Auxiliary for the Organizationally Impaired, I'm also the spokesperson for Overtalkers Anonymous—an association that's clearly not anonymous at all since we talk so much.

The conversation traveled to deep topics including heaven and life in light of eternity. When you have friends dying, it's hard to not land there when someone asks how things are going. Sure an everything's-fine pleasantry would be sufficient, but why not be honest. I've been so moved at my friends' newfound level of purpose and relationship and urgency coupled with dialed-down, all-things-shallow approach to life since their days have been numbered—it's inspiring.

He shared with me that a few years ago his twin brother had been diagnosed with cancer. "It's funny," he told me, "when you hear a diagnosis like that, life suddenly gets put into perspective—especially since there was a high likelihood that I would receive the same diagnosis being that we're identical."

He did not get diagnosed, and after treatment, his brother was fine. But during that time, life changed. Peripheral things didn't matter as much, possessions lost their lure. Attaining an abundance of things took a backseat to time, which gained a new importance. It became more about time together with family and friends.

"During that period, my life completely slowed down. I said no to almost everything. The moments—good, bad, and everything in between—mattered more than anything else. It was wonderful," he told me. "It's hard to believe that with a dire situation, stress was completely dialed down. In fact, just talking about it makes me wish I could go back to that trimmed-down way of life."

Jen said the same thing. "One of the gifts of suffering is the detachment from things that we cling to, but don't really matter. The world doesn't have much to offer people who suffer. Consequently, it's hard to not look to the next and be excited for the life where everything—want or need—is met in unimaginable abundance."

She concluded, "In heaven I won't struggle with control and with perfectionism—my major issues here. So, when I struggle here, why not allow the Truth to inform. When we're overcome by stress that is legitimate or significant things like suffering or loss or when we're overcome by anxiety over our schedule that is just not going our way—replay the Truth: this world is not my home and this stuff just won't be in heaven."

If a pronouncement of numbered days inspires people to make the most of their moments, why not be inspired today since we're all in the same boat—even if our days don't have a specific number? What would it be like if they did? Why even consider eternity or allow it to weigh in? How can it inform our thoughts, actions, our perspective, our conversations and relationships today? My friend Janet Denison says,

> Maybe we won't notice what is broken and focus instead on what will last forever. Maybe we won't be overly concerned with our physical health and will make our spiritual health a higher priority. Maybe we won't think about our bank statement as much as our treasure in heaven. Maybe we won't fret over temporal fears on earth and choose instead to find peace in our eternal promises.[5]

Water Station

PRACTICING ETERNAL PERSPECTIVE

In 2011, *The Guardian* followed four people who had terminal diagnoses. What is it like? How has knowing life will likely end soon affected life today? One of the people lives angry. Interestingly, he is the only person living life alone. Another, a twenty-five-year-old, said she would not go back to the days pre-diagnosis since her life has changed so much for the better.

"I've gained a perspective on life that is a gift in all its rawness. I'm really quite grateful for that even though the circumstances are awful," says Holly Webber.

> What's cruel about this illness is that I've been given a time limit. Life is so precious and we all believe we're invincible, but I know what's happening to my body. Somebody asked me recently how I cope with despair, and the only answer that I could come up with is that what keeps me going is the hope that everything will somehow be OK. I've been told I have a terminal illness, and I get that, but if I didn't wake up every morning hopeful, then I wouldn't get out of bed, get dressed, eat or breathe. What's anyone without hope?
>
> Sometimes I feel like I'm on another planet looking in on this one. I can't relate to people stressing about work or getting the Tube. People are so wound up, but it's such a waste of time and energy. Chill out! I hope that by reading this, someone out there will take a second to think . . . maybe I should worry less about the things that don't really matter.[6]

If technically speaking we all have the same diagnosis—most of us without a specific number attached—why not practice living today with a little less momentary and a lot more eternal, purposefilled perspective?

196

twelve

Rather Than Be Overwhelmed by *Any* Trappings of This World, Be Overwhelmed by Hope

> Hope is like the sun, which, as we journey toward it, casts the shadow of our burden behind us.
>
> Samuel Smiles

That sad January day, the day we celebrated a life ended early, I looked at the row of girls. More than one would come up to me after the funeral, asking if B's death was their fault.

Hundreds of kids in long rows, though surrounded by peers, struggled with feeling alone—the alone-in-a-crowd feeling that kids, all of us if we're honest, know too well.

As I looked at the beautiful place of worship, I saw a minister deeply grieved by the course of action, families somber from the loss, a soloist fighting the overwhelming emotion of it all to find her voice. An impressive backdrop dwarfed the discreet pine casket at the foot of the stage. An inscription of God's Ten Commandments—a reminder of what needs to be done in order to be okay—hung on the wall.

Not the Boss of Us

I looked again at the row where I sat. Then my eyes scanned the crowd as they traveled back to the Ten Commandments displayed so clearly. I couldn't help but think that religion likely played and plays a part in Overwhelmed.

How can anyone live up to those standards? Knowing B the little that I did, I'm sure she tried. Don't we all struggle under the pressures to be and to do in so many areas of life, but especially in religion where there is eternity to think about?

I thought about the weight I had felt in my own life from that looming list that was impossible to achieve the minute it was written—literally in stone.

I've had a love-hate relationship with the Ten Commandments. I love that it sets out specific steps of action—do these things and you're in. But I hate that the list is basically impossible—let alone adding to the mix an all-day, everyday deal that makes it a bit overwhelming.

For B, the seemingly endless pressures and stress in her life were enough to convince a kid to check out. But add the centuries old list that has something to do with eternity—that's heavy stuff.

But as I looked again at that list of commandments so prominently placed, I was truly overwhelmed.

Not by the rules. Not by the right way. Not by the enormity of religious measuring marks that actually are unattainable.

No, I was overwhelmed with gratitude. I was overwhelmed by love and grace. Overwhelmed by mercy. Overwhelmed that those laws, though never abolished, were fulfilled. And I prayed, in the midst of that tragic scene—mourning the death of a life that had only just begun, so many of the kids wondering if something they had said or done caused it—God would help each of us somehow wade through the sorrow, the doubt, the pain, the anger, the loss, and the countless unknowns to understand what *finished*—as in "It is finished"[1]—and *fulfilled* mean.

What if the words "It is finished," uttered by Jesus as he died on the cross in order to give life to grace and mercy, actually meant

198

It was finished for good—not finished in heaven, or finished for a moment, but finished on earth that day and forevermore? What if *It* meant death including all the trappings of this world that masquerade as life but actually kill. What if *It is finished* reached forward and backward, victorious over all death—physical death, death that comes with broken relationship, death that comes with aging, death that accompanies every stress and pressure that steals life and joy from the people upon which it preys.

We can't always see how such victory plays out, but what if that victory is more real than what we do see? According to theologian N. T. Wright, the fact that *It is finished* means "done" just might be the part of the story we forget to see or hear or embrace.

> In the West we have been so seduced by the Platonic vision of "heaven" that the resurrection of Jesus is seen simply as the "happy ending" after the crucifixion, and as the prelude to his "going to heaven" so that we can go and join him there later. This misses the central point that the resurrection of Jesus is *the beginning of the new creation, in which we are to share already in the power of the Spirit.* This affects everything.[2]

If *It is finished* means "done," why not allow it to inform the stresses and pressures of today? Why not be overwhelmed by that? In order to do that, we must trust without being able to see with our eyes or touch with our hands—a.k.a. faith.

Wonderful, Horrible Faith

Sometimes, on special days, I stop by Eatzi's, a terrific local take-out market, and grab a sandwich and a large ice tea to go. Eatzi's always has taste stations scattered around the store for patrons to test their goods. Deep River's Zesty Jalapeno chips were available last week.

I ate three.

I got my sandwich and circled back by the chip bowl, pretended to be intrigued, and "tasted" them again. This time I took five.

Then I bought a bag.

Oh my word, they are so delicious. Seriously. Those chips are a party in your mouth. They're so wonderful and horrible at the same time. They trick you into thinking they're a regular chip. But about halfway through chewing, the fire starts. It's so hot. It burns but doesn't consume. It leaves your mouth smoking for several minutes—a reminder of their presence, or maybe a little take-home gift. Their heat is balanced with perfect saltiness and yummy chip goodness.

As I munched through the bag, literally sweating from the heat, trading agony with pleasure, I considered how those chips, though far from a perfect illustration, reminded me of faith.

I'm convinced that faith, next to grace, is one of the most special gifts that God has given us. It is a vehicle to special intimacy. Faith—being sure of what we hope for and certain of what we don't see[3]—puts into practice our trust in God. Through faith, we act on what we know to be true, even when circumstances tempt us to think otherwise. The fire in those chips reminded me (yet again) what God said through the prophet Isaiah:

> But now, this is what the LORD says—
>   he who created you, Jacob,
>   he who formed you, Israel:
> "Do not fear, for I have redeemed you;
>   I have summoned you by name; you are mine.
> When you pass through the waters,
>   I will be with you;
> and when you pass through the rivers,
>   they will not sweep over you.
> When you walk through the fire,
> you will not be burned;
>   the flames will not set you ablaze.

> For I am the LORD your God,
>   the Holy One of Israel, your Savior."[4]

What a beautiful promise, so sweet and wonderful. I want to lean into every aspect of it. Do I believe it? I mean really believe?

The promise sounds good—until I'm living a circumstance that leads me to chew on those words and feel the fire. But like those chips, whose heat burns my mouth, the goodness that comes with such trust is wonderful, even in the midst of hardship, as we lean into God's promise that we will "walk through the fire" and "not be burned." Because he says so. Because his Word is true.

God even went beyond figurative speech to literally show us the truth of his promise. In the third chapter in the book of Daniel, some boys lived through a fiery furnace moment, emerging unscathed, no hair singed, not even a hint of a smoky smell.

Because God is Lord over all, no circumstance is above him.

Still, circumstances exist.

But the hard, undoable, take-your-breath-away, I'm-not-sure-I-can-make-it stuff that really forces us to lean into the "sure of what we hope for" and the "certain of what we cannot see" just might be the best (and the worst) part of our relationship with God. These circumstances take us to the place where we must trust *and* believe. And in doing so, a special intimacy occurs since we can't do it on our own.

Interestingly, the angels have never had faith. They've always been able to see God's goodness—his goodness on the outside. And when we stand before the Lord, faith will no longer play a role in our relationship either. We will see with our eyes and know.

But today we live by faith. Have we been given this wonderful (yet horrible) gift of faith so that we can tap into unseen goodness, goodness that is within God that can be known only by trusting him? I don't know. But I do know that there are some circumstances that we just can't make it through on our own. And I guess that's where trust and faith again play their role.

Because what do you do when you're watching the ten o'clock local news and the lead story is about a horrible car accident on Northwest Highway close to your house? What do you do when the car in that crash looks familiar? What do you do when you look at the clock and wonder why your seventeen-year-old son who called about twenty-five minutes ago from a location fifteen minutes away isn't home when he just told you he was headed that way? What do you do when the realization of what's going on is too much to handle? It just can't be true. He just called. He's on his way home. But it's *his* car swallowed in flames leading the evening news.

It's too much.

My friends Taylor and Jennifer who experienced just that and, with their hearts still breaking, stand firm—not on their own foundation but on the One who never wavers, whose provision is always sufficient, even when circumstances beg us to fear otherwise. The struggle to put one foot in front of the other isn't as hard as it was five years ago when they lost their son. Literally, with each step, they have stood strong in their faith. Joyful, truly joyful, while crying at the same time.

Joy in the midst of pain is exemplified through this sentiment that Taylor shared with me. "Words just don't capture the deep, deep level of pain felt and the glory of God realized as he lifted us from that pain—not immediately, but in his sovereignty over the time period he deems perfect as he continues to lift us." In the midst of unimaginable heartache, they stand equally unimaginably overwhelmed by Truth.

And therein lies the mystery: How can something as wonderful as faith—sinking into all the goodness of God's sufficiency, provision, and love—be so horrible at the same time? Trusting that God has it covered is hard. *What an understatement.* But almost inexplicable good abounds in the midst of such trust.

I'm thankful that God never said we must go it alone. I guess that's another interesting aspect of faith: relationship.

> So do not fear, for I am with you;
>> do not be dismayed, for I am your God.
> I will strengthen you and help you;
>> I will uphold you with my righteous right hand.[5]

To experience God's sustenance and promise—undeniable. To live through the challenging day-to-day—agonizing. Wonderful, horrible faith. Faith that finds life in hope.

Hope

It's amazing to me how a smell or sight or sound can send my stomach into a pit of ache. Today when attempting to lighten the storage load on my phone, I saw and couldn't stop myself from reading a text I had received from Jen before she died.

Friend.

I always loved how she would offer an assessment, a declaration of sorts rather than a name. No one else does that in my life. It was her deal. I miss it. Just seeing that simple statement brought with it a familiar sting of tears.

You're good to me. Thanks for entering into the brutal honesty and unknowns of my world. I am thankful when friends can "go there" with us. Scott has said his greatest blessing is hearing how others feel about it and when they walk this road with us by sharing their own feelings and experiences. And you did that. Beautifully as always. I love you friend.

I miss her. I'm sad she's gone. And I'm surprised at how quickly my eyes can cloud and my chest can tighten. Even though it's simply a relationship interruption.

Still, I don't like good-byes. Really any of them. I especially don't like good-byes of the long-term variety.

I had sat next to Jen at a lively little gathering and had the conversation which had prompted her text.

We had talked about a looming good-bye. Her looming good-bye. Which was weird. It's strange to talk to someone whose body is being ravaged from the inside out with cancer. It was like she was going on a trip, but she didn't know when she was leaving. So until the plane was ready to board, she was making the very most of every moment—all while fighting to stay alive.

I loved our chat and her brutal honesty. I loved watching her sink into all the goodness of time with friends. I was so thankful to get to meet several of her sister-friends whom, until then, I had known only by name. And I loved watching God tenderly carry this faithful daughter along the most challenging of roads in the loveliest way.

I watched Jen and her friends laugh and reminisce and simply enjoy being together. Most of them lived apart, as we all do from many friends throughout the different stages of our lives. No one was letting her sickness cast a shadow on time together. Because the beauty of time spent well is in our friendships.

I thought about good-byes while watching everyone. Why are good-byes so hard? Why do they hurt? Why does it feel like a part of ourselves is being ripped away when those we love say good-bye?

The truth is I don't think we were made for good-byes. I think pretty much just the opposite. We were made for togetherness.

In the book I've been reading, *Surprised by Oxford*, Carolyn Weber recounts a dinner at the esteemed university where she sat next to a renowned heart surgeon from the United States named Dr. Inchbald. Being that the physician's field put him in countless life-and-death situations, he was asked by another guest about his view on God, science, and life. A portion of his response, an aha moment he had while literally holding someone's heart, resonated with me.

> "Well, as I was standing there, all the uncertainty of my life, the absurdity of all this death, and all our attempts to ward it off, came down to a pinprick of light—like the glint off the scalpel in my hand. . . .
>
> "I've come to the conclusion that God is sovereign, even over science, and that I cannot pretend to fully know His ways. They really are mysterious, as the saying goes. And they are not of the mind of men, no matter how hard we try to wrap our minds about these ways. . . . But to cut to the chase," Dr. Inchbald stated, "when I see death, I know it is wrong."
>
> "Obviously." Dr. Rieland snickered.
>
> "But *really, really wrong*. In-my-gut wrong," Dr. Inchbald almost pleaded. "It was not meant to be. It was not meant for us. We were not built for it. Everything in my body, at a cellular level, let alone a metaphysical one, twists against it. Not just *my* death, but the death of every living thing."[6]

I think he has a point.

Of late, I've had more than enough illness and looming long-term separation surrounding me and my friends. Each case has caused me pause—sometimes debilitating pause. And I've thought about Dr. Inchbald's "wrong" comment. And I've thought back to the beginning when the words "It is not good for the man to be alone"[7] were said. It's a statement that sparked a new being and companionship. Man was created in God's image—the Trinity, the epitome of relationship. Creation itself points to our innate need for relationship, togetherness.

Maybe that's why separation hurts so much.

Maybe that's why good-byes are so hard.

I found myself talking with Snopes yesterday about relationship after we saw some people arguing in one of the university orientation lines. It was like a tiny little death between those two people. Even though it would be short lived, unlike a last breath, it was disturbing.

Relationship isn't meant for brokenness.

Which made us think about brokenness and how unsettling it is. There are so many things that cause or invite brokenness into relationship. And we feel, physically feel, bad until things are restored. Then we wondered if that's why Christ cried out, "Why have you forsaken me?"[8] when relationship was broken with God, who is the essence of relationship. He *is* relationship, forever connected, forever serving, uplifting, walking alongside the other.

Overwhelmed by Immensity:
A SMALL PROJECT, A BIG IDEA

When sisters Katherine and Isabelle Adams were five and eight years old, they learned that millions of people in the world do not have access to clean drinking water. This knowledge had a profound impact on them, and they decided they wanted to make a difference. They made handcrafted origami that they would exchange for donations to build a water well for a community in Ethiopia. With this decision in 2011, Paper for Water was founded.

In that original project, their goal was to raise five hundred dollars. After it was completed, they had raised almost ten thousand dollars. Since then, they haven't stopped. To date, these two girls, who are now eleven and fourteen, have worked with hundreds of volunteers to raise over a million dollars and have helped fund over one hundred and forty water projects in fourteen countries, including Ethiopia, Ghana, Kenya, Liberia, India, Mexico, Uganda, Peru, and Zimbabwe.

Then we thought about that broken aspect and the role it played in redemption so that we could have the Holy Spirit—absolute intimacy with God as he lives in us—a mystery as Dr. Inchbald might say.

And we were humbled and grateful and wondered if the broken part of relationship here is to remind us of the restoration secured for us through Christ.

Good-byes are sad.

But one thing we know with certainty since God says these things about himself: he redeems. He is love, and he knows and understands and restores. He has experienced brokenness, the relationship interruption too. What if, in the Garden of Gethsemane, as Jesus was soon to be ushered to trial, condemnation,

At age eleven, Katherine was one of the keynote speakers for the Big Room at the National Youth Workers' Convention in 2017. Her words are sure to inspire us as much as they did the cheering crowd.

It doesn't matter how old or young you are. Everybody wants to make a difference in the world. But some people just get overwhelmed by the immensity of the world's problems and just don't start. But with Paper for Water we focus on bringing water and the Word to the thirsty one piece of paper at a time. And one piece of paper is manageable. We have realized that the thirsty are not just in developing countries but are right here in our own city: thirsty for meaning; thirsty to help; thirsty to know they have made a difference.[9]

The problems of this world can seem and feel like too much. But rather than shut down and be overwhelmed by the enormity of issues ranging from geopolitical divide all the way to deep personal issues, why not be overwhelmed by the Truth that we only have to take one step, offer one drink of water at a time?

and death, he was so deeply saddened in part due to pending physical separation from us? Because he would miss us. No longer able to touch, literally physically touch, and audibly speak or laugh with the people he loved? I wouldn't be surprised—although we are often surprised at the idea that relationship with us could be so precious.

I don't know how he did it, but in his conquering of death, Jesus restored everything that is broken, everything that death has touched. And he gives peace through hope—absolute and certain—whether we can see it or not.

And here's where we come face-to-face with all the pressures and stresses of the world that overwhelm us. Reaching for truth, in light of eternity, those things have nothing on us. Literally nothing. They're little Nerf pellets. They're like annoying little fleas to be flicked away. With Truth on our side—seeing the landscape with God-centered, far-sighted vision—we can, in the most mysterious way, actually experience Truth in our souls with all its grace and hope and peace and joy.

So why not take sips from the living water so we can be fully hydrated, soul hydrated, ready to travel life's road—hills and all.

And reach for hope that goes so much farther than grief.

Hope gently lifts, steadily adjusts, and brings truth into focus. Hope shines light. It holds back the floods and the storms so that the waters don't rise over. It blocks the flames so they don't burn. It shelters and keeps us safe. It protects and sets us up high upon a rock (an unmovable and unshakable rock) planted upon the firmest foundation. It always sees and always knows and has defeated every foe through which grief finds traction.

Love

"Don't worry," Barton encouraged me after I had come back from caring for a friend who was dealing with extreme grief, months after her husband's passing. "She's going to be okay." It had now been close to a year since B died.

"Why do you say that?" I ask. She said it with such steady assurance, I wanted to know how she could be so sure. What was informing her perspective to a point that she could definitively declare such a thing.

"The doubt, the frustration, the being mad at God—so mad. I mean if God is real and loving, how could he let B die like that? I hated God. Wow, I can't believe I said that out loud," she admitted, shaking her head and slightly smiling. "Despite *all* of that, God never moved or left and never seemed to ask more from me than to trust him. I just can't believe how kind he is. And that he would endure all of the bad things that are screamed his way—just so we can know his kindness and love and complete acceptance. Who does that?"

Then she said something matter-of-factly yet emphatically, "The doubt actually increased my faith."

Wow.

Doubt led her to question, which led her to seek and to search and to test which road to travel. Is it the world's performance/measuring-up way, the world's do-or-die way, the world's pay to play way, the world's appearances matter way, the world's now or never way, the world's everyone's watching way? Or is it trusting beyond what can be seen since none of those things are the boss of us way. Truth is, a fifteen-year-old chose to bank on Truth.

Barton sat next to me. "How can God love me so much?" Then, again shaking her head, this time with a huge smile, she said, "I can barely believe it."

I actually think that's where we go off the tracks or never get on. How can we even know or grasp unconditional love, the kind where you don't have to do or to be something in order to get it. What does that love even look like? I recently bumped into and was floored by something I've read more than once but have never

209

seen. The Lord speaking through Isaiah said, "You are precious and honored in my sight, and . . . I love you."[10] Do we believe that? Maybe that's why the apostle Paul begged:

> And I pray that you, being rooted and established in love, may have power, together with all the Lord's holy people, to grasp how wide and long and high and deep is the love of Christ, and to know this love that surpasses knowledge."[11]

It filled my heart that this young lady beside me was allowing herself to be loved like that. Rather than give the trappings of this world an inch, she was reaching to be overwhelmed by Truth with all its grace and love and hope and peace. The Truth that she has nothing to prove. The Truth that she can live life fully known, fully loved, and free to be all that she was created to be.

And I've watched her step in to stop friends from listening or buying into the do-all/be-all pressures that hit them every day.

"Your worth isn't tied to that grade. Who cares if it was bad?" she recently urged her friend Cate who, like Barton, works hard to do her best. "Don't let one bad grade take away from all the other good ones."

"It was a zero," her friend lamented back, saying out loud something she refused to voice minutes before.

"Wow, that is bad," Barton said. No faking. No coddling. Which maybe made her response believable. And helped Cate reframe. Only after gently asking and reminding her that "it will be okay" did she reply to Barton's sincere "Are you okay?"

"I know I can do a retake," Cate said. "Sure the cap is a seventy, but anything is better than a zero." This time she chuckled as she said the word out loud again.

We cannot tame Overwhelmed by ourselves. Cate was brave enough to answer Barton's question. Barton, looking up, could see a hurting person traveling alongside her, and she wanted to know what was messing with her friend. Their friend B couldn't say the words out loud—whatever words and mismessaging duped her into believing a lie about her self-worth.

I had a hard time saying the words when I was their age. Thankfully, something stopped me when I was in college and I could no longer function with my coping strategies to deal with stress, pressures, and expectations amidst all the cultural mismessaging that I heard and bought into. I look back and know that God, in the mysterious yet undeniable way that he works, redirected me.

For example, in the strangest way, during that period every time I got in my car a radio advertisement came on for an eating disorder program in Dallas. Not only had I never heard an ad like that before, I have never heard another since. Encouraged that a place existed to give a tired soul a hand up, I reached out. But that only went so far seeing that upon completion of that program, I was hit with the "your pants look a little tight" comment. But it didn't end there. Again in the most unlikely way, our friend Chuck Bentley, now with Crown Financial Ministry, reached out to my folks and offered me a job at Discipleship Counseling Services until I went back to school. Day in and day out, I did big things like stuffing envelopes or making copies while Chuck and a man named Bob George simply spoke Truth over me. Though I had attended church my entire life, I had somehow missed the message about God's love and mercy and grace—for me, for us.

My life was forever changed by that. I've never gone back to buying into the world's messaging. Granted, I didn't use the exact words that I might find myself yelling to my kids as they walk out the door now:

- There is no right way—your decision to take a different path is fine, even great—right-way isn't the boss of you.
- The group thing is just a group—it's not the boss, there's a seat for you, always. Which, by the way, proved true for

Fury, who walked from the cafeteria line with his tray and sat with some super nice seniors. Who would have thought?

- You're beautiful, you have a unique body type, and you're never a victim to trends!
- Performance does not define who you are—you're a person, not a product or a persona—please don't ever let it make you think you need to get on a treadmill to nowhere.
- You are *you-nique* with purpose and gifting as individual to you as a your fingerprint.

But for all intents and purposes, I had called out all the world's trappings—including religion's right way of doing things, which is very different from relationship firmly anchored in grace through faith—and emphatically declared that they were absolutely not the boss of me (or anyone for that matter) anymore.

It warms my heart to no end seeing people I love hearing, believing, and sharing that message with people traveling alongside them. Leaving no stone unturned with Cate, Barton adds for good measure, "And no matter what, that grade doesn't change who you are as a person."

If nothing else, her walking alongside and meeting a significant blip helped stop the hemorrhaging. Their choosing to hear Truth over societal messaging that could easily dupe anyone into seeing themselves as a non-rehabilitatable failure made the ground stable.

It's a choice available to all of us. Life's pressures and stress and expectations and even hard circumstances in whatever walk of life we find ourselves just aren't the boss of us.

If a teenager, knowing, not fearing—okay maybe a little fearing—that there's still a lot of ground to be covered on her journey in life can arrive at such a conclusion—choosing to remember and stay grounded in Truth on the road ahead—well, enough said.

Acknowledgments

Thank you begins with my family. I don't just love my kids and husband, but I really *like* them—so much more than they will ever know. They make life fun to live in both bright and dim times. They keep it real, don't run from hard, see beauty in the big and small, admit fears, get angry, apologize, and extend an open invitation to laughter during it all. Words can't begin to describe the amount of admiration I feel for these people. I am honored to know them, let alone to live life with them. And they're nice to put up with my sharing our stories in an effort to remind ourselves and encourage others as we travel life's roads.

Thanks to Wolgemuth & Associates for going alongside me. A special thanks to Erik Wolgemuth for all the many ways you help, offer wisdom, put up with my fire hydrant stream of ideas, listen to me ramble, and provide endless encouragement.

Thanks to the wonderful folks at Revell, especially Andrea Doering—you had me at "I love how Overwhelmed is personified"— Wendy Wetzel, Robin Turici, and the marketing/PR gang. I've not only appreciated the hard work and commitment on this book but I am especially grateful for the kind words of encouragement and new friendships.

Thanks to my friends who have put up with me *not-the-boss*-ing about everything: Mandy Bagdanov, Candy Hill, Tracey Murtha, Ann Silva, Betsy Nowlin, Charla Autrey, Mary Clayton Wood, Nell Bush, Lynn Campbell, Jane Jarrell, Chris Wills, Lynne Schott, Erin Schreyer, Brenda Teele, Courtney DeFeo, Kari Stainback, Elizabeth Stuart, and honestly a host of others including Jennifer Clouse and Greg Murtha who are living the *long tomorrow* today.

A special thanks to Julie and Nancy and the Lovell-Fairchild gang for all you have done over the last few years to get the word out. I can't help but thank Laura Barker for taking a chance on a new writer who wasn't sure she was a writer and for showing me the ropes.

Thanks to all my *MOATblog*, *SaySomething Show*, and Neighborhood Studies friends who have walked the road with me—it sure would be a lonely adventure without you!

And I have to bookend the thanks with my family. To my mom and dad, Sue and Don Wills, for being a never-ending source of encouragement. To my siblings, David, Kathy, and Charles—and the in-laws Chris, Don, and Paula—who are there for me when I call. And thanks to Dick Wyma, for being a steady source of inspiration and encouragement.

If there is any truth or wisdom in this book, it isn't mine. I'm just along for the ride. All wisdom within is supplied by the Author of Truth. He has so much more to share and gives generously without finding fault (see James 1). Check it out sometime. We read the New International Version (1984) around our house.

Notes

Chapter 1 The Beginning of the End of Overwhelmed as We Knew It

1. See *Merriam-Webster Unabridged*, "overwhelm," accessed April 30, 2018, https://www.merriam-webster.com/dictionary/overwhelm.

2. Luis Ferré-Sadurní, "'Overwhelmed' Postal Carrier Hoarded 17,000 Pieces of Mail, Officials Say," *New York Times*, April 21, 2018, https://www.nytimes.com/2018/04/21/nyregion/undelivered-mail-hoarded.html.

3. See *Vocabulary.com*, "persona," accessed February 28, 2018, https://www.vocabulary.com/dictionary/persona.

4. Tim Keller, *The Meaning of Marriage: Facing the Complexities of Commitment with the Wisdom of God* (New York: Penguin Books, 2015), 95.

5. Brené Brown, "Listening to Shame," filmed at TED2012, TED Conferences, LLC, video, https://www.ted.com/talks/brene_brown_listening_to_shame/transcript#t-1218994.

Chapter 2 Rather Than Be Overwhelmed by Performance Pressures, Be Overwhelmed by Purpose

1. Alex Lickerman, "Why Perfect Is the Enemy of Good," *Psychology Today*, June 26, 2011, https://www.psychologytoday.com/blog/happiness-in-world/201106/why-perfect-is-the-enemy-good.

2. "SaySomething Carpool Diem with Shauna Niequist on Perfectionism, Togetherness & Belonging," YouTube video, posted by "Kay Wyma," September 29, 2016, https://www.youtube.com/watch?v=kaAbiMPEhQQ.

3. "Carpool Diem with Shauna Niequist," YouTube.

4. Corbett Smith, "Back to the 1600s," *Dallas News*, March 2016, https://www.dallasnews.com/news/news/2016/03/04/back-to-the-1600s-the-new-sat-makes-big-changes-shaves-off-the-essay-and-students-seem-to-dig-it.

5. Smith, "Back to the 1600s."

215

6. Wolfgang Riebe, *100 Quotes to Make You Think!* (Mind Power Publications, 2010).

7. "Poet & Author Amena Brown on Fixing Our Broken-Record Self Messaging," YouTube video, posted by "Kay Wyma," November 11, 2017, https://www.youtube.com/watch?v=N00ocNnevTU.

Chapter 3 Rather Than Be Overwhelmed by Appearance Pressures, Be Overwhelmed by Beauty

1. Eugene Lee Yang, Mark Celestino, and Kari Koeppel, "Women's Ideal Body Types Throughout History," BuzzFeed video, January 27, 2015, https://www.buzzfeed.com/eugeneyang/womens-ideal-body-types-throughout-history?utm_term=.snkPvOx17#.ssW640VB2.

2. Amanda Foreman, "Why Footbinding Persisted in China for a Millenium," *Smithsonian.com*, February 2015, https://www.smithsonianmag.com/history/why-footbinding-persisted-china-millennium-180953971/#HRlKHtbEMvhmtP9w.99.

3. "Natural Skin Care Products," Frownies: The Original Wrinkle Patch, accessed April 30, 2018, https://www.frownies.com/.

4. Alanna Vagianos, "Dove's 'Choose Beautiful' Campaign Says Women Are So Much More Than Average," *Huffington Post*, April 7, 2015, https://www.huffingtonpost.com/2015/04/07/dove-beauty-choose-beautiful-campaign-video_n_7010178.html.

5. "Sustainable Diet & Exercise with Meredith Boyd," YouTube video, posted by "Kay Wyma," January 10, 2017, https://www.youtube.com/watch?v=u86ctaZHq5Y.

6. "SaySomething - Bobby Rodriguez on Faith, Fitness & Health," YouTube video, posted by "Kay Wyma," September 14, 2016, https://www.youtube.com/watch?v=C6e_Xarcls8.

7. Ronnie Koenig, "13-Year-Old Girl's Inspiring Viral Poem Tells Teens: 'You Are Good Enough,'" *Today*, June 2, 2017, https://www.today.com/parents/girl-s-inspiring-poem-tells-teens-you-are-good-enough-t112175.

8. Koenig, "You Are Good Enough."

9. Koenig, "You Are Good Enough.

Chapter 4 Rather Than Be Overwhelmed by Image Pressures, Be Overwhelmed by Image Bearing

1. Keith Perry, "One in Five Children Just Want to Be Rich When They Grow Up," *Telegraph*, August 5, 2014, http://www.telegraph.co.uk/news/newstopics/howaboutthat/11014591/One-in-five-children-just-want-to-be-rich-when-they-grow-up.html.

2. Peter Tait, "Fame and Fortune Should Not Be Our Children's Only Ambitions in Life," *Telegraph*, February 5, 2016, http://www.telegraph.co.uk/education/2016/03/14/fame-and-fortune-should-not-be-our-childrens-only-ambitions-in-l/.

3. Quoted in Kelly McEvers, "Don't Be Fooled: 'Generation Wealth' Is More about Wanting than Having," NPR, May 10, 2017, http://www.npr.org/2017

/05/10/527429299/dont-be-fooled-generation-wealth-is-more-about-wanting
-than-having.

4. McEvers, "Don't Be Fooled."

5. McEvers, "Don't Be Fooled."

6. *Notting Hill*, directed by Robert Mitchell (Universal City, CA: Universal, 1999).

7. *Notting Hill*, Universal.

8. Kate Fagan, "Split Image," *ESPNW*, May 7, 2015, http://www.espn.com/espn
/feature/story/_/id/12833146/instagram-account-university-pennsylvania-runner
-showed-only-part-story.

9. Mother Teresa, "A Message for the World Conference on Women, Beijing,
China," Gifts of Speech, September 1995, http://gos.sbc.edu/m/mothert2.html.

10. C. S. Lewis, *The Weight of Glory* (New York: HarperOne, 1949), 46.

11. Lauren Gambino, "Harvard's Prestigious Debate Team Loses to New
York Prison Inmates," *Guardian*, October 7, 2015, https://www.theguardian.com
/education/2015/oct/07/harvards-prestigious-debate-team-loses-to-new-york
-prison-inmates.

12. Henri Nouwen, *Life of the Beloved: Spiritual Living in a Secular World*
(New York: Crossroad Publishing Company, 2002), 57.

Chapter 5 Rather Than Be Overwhelmed by Formulaic Right-Way Pressures, Be Overwhelmed by Perfect Imperfection

1. Originally published in slightly different form in Joslyn Taylor, "Kay Wyma
On Being Perfectly Imperfect," *DMagazine (Family)*, January 14, 2013, https://
www.dmagazine.com/family/2013/01/kay-wyma-on-being-perfectly-imperfect/.
Reprinted by permission of the author and the publisher.

2. See *Merriam-Webster Unabridged*, "rubric," accessed February 15, 2018,
http://unabridged.merriam-webster.com/unabridged/rubric.

3. Taylor, "Kay Wyma On Being Perfectly Imperfect."

4. Lee Smolin, "Einstein's Lonely Path," *Discover*, September 30, 2004, http://
discovermagazine.com/2004/sep/einsteins-lonely-path.

5. Robert Adams, "48 Famous Failures Who Will Inspire You to Achieve,"
Wanderlust Worker (blog), https://www.wanderlustworker.com/48-famous-failures
-who-will-inspire-you-to-achieve/.

6. Donald Miller, *A Million Miles in a Thousand Years: What I Learned While
Editing My Life* (Nashville: Thomas Nelson, 2009), 206.

7. Originally published in slightly different form in Kay Wyma, "4 Things to
Remember about Dashed Expectations," *Boundless* (blog), *Focus on the Family*,
November 6, 2015, http://www.boundless.org/blog/4-things-to-remember-about
-dashed-expectations/. Reprinted by permission of the author and the publisher.

Chapter 6 Rather Than Be Overwhelmed by Group Pressures, Be Overwhelmed by Belonging

1. Neel Burton, MD, "Our Hierarchy of Needs," *Psychology Today*, May 23, 2012,
https://www.psychologytoday.com/blog/hide-and-seek/201205/our-hierarchy-needs.

2. Amanda Lenhart, "Teens, Social Media, and Technology Overview 2015," Pew Research Center, April 9, 2015, http://www.pewinternet.org/2015/04/09/teens-social-media-technology-2015/#teens.
3. Maeve Duggan, Amanda Lenhart, Cliff Lampe, and Nicole B. Ellison, "Parents and Social Media," Pew Research Center, July 16, 2015, http://www.pewinternet.org/2015/07/16/parents-and-social-media/.
4. John Steinbeck, *The Winter of Our Discontent* (New York: Viking Press, 1961).
5. Dale Carnegie, *How to Win Friends and Influence People* (New York: Pocket Books, 1936), 105.
6. Isa. 43:1–3.

Chapter 7 Rather Than Be Overwhelmed by Do-All Pressures, Be Overwhelmed by the Sacred in the Ordinary

1. Shankar Vedantam, "Instead of Showing Off Wealth, Some Show Off Busy Schedules," NPR, April 27, 2017, http://www.npr.org/2017/04/27/525833226/instead-of-showing-off-wealth-some-show-off-busy-schedules.
2. Brigid Schulte, "Insanely Busy Schedules Are the New Status Symbol," *Dallas News*, April 2014, https://www.dallasnews.com/opinion/commentary/2014/04/04/insanely-busy-schedules-are-the-new-status-symbol.
3. Greg McKeown, *Essentialism* (New York: Crown Business, 2014), 68.
4. Stuart Jeffries, "Why Too Much Choice Is Stressing Us Out," *Guardian*, October 2015, https://www.theguardian.com/lifeandstyle/2015/oct/21/choice-stressing-us-out-dating-partners-monopolies.
5. Jeffries, "Why Too Much Choice is Stressing Us Out," 2015.
6. Jackie Bledsoe, "Whiteboard Quote of the Day: 'Trees That Are Slow to Grow, Bear the Best Fruit," *Jackie Bledsoe* (blog), August 4, 2012, http://jackiebledsoe.com/whiteboard-quote-of-the-day-trees-that-are-slow-to-grow-bear-the-best-fruit/.
7. Amy Morrin, "Seven Scientifically Proven Benefits of Gratitude That Will Motivate You to Give Thanks Year-Round," *Forbes*, November 23, 2014, https://www.forbes.com/sites/amymorin/2014/11/23/7-scientifically-proven-benefits-of-gratitude-that-will-motivate-you-to-give-thanks-year-round/#1a6dc8c1183c.

Chapter 8 Rather Than Be Overwhelmed by Product Pressures, Be Overwhelmed by the Process

1. "Perspective-Laced Wisdom on Life & Kids with Jeff Hendricks," YouTube video, 4:32, posted by "Kay Wyma," September 27, 2017, https://www.youtube.com/watch?v=NLXNViRcu-s.
2. Malcolm Gladwell, *David and Goliath: Underdogs, Misfits, and the Art of Battling Giants* (Boston: Little, Brown, 2013), 9–11.
3. "Memory and Senses," *Puls*, accessed March 1, 2018, http://grimstad.uia.no/puls/studystrategy/mne08/03mne08.htm.

Chapter 9 Rather Than Be Overwhelmed by Circumstances, Be Overwhelmed by Looking Up

1. NBC 5 Staff, "Sniper Ambush Kills 5 Officers, Injures 7 in Dallas Following Peaceful Protest," *NBCDFW.com*, July 7, 2016, https://www.nbcdfw.com/news /local/Protests-in-Dallas-Over-Alton-Sterling-Death-385784431.html.

2. Fred Rogers, *The Mister Rogers' Parenting Book* (Philadelphia: Running Press, 2002), 107.

3. Martin Luther King Jr., *The Papers of Martin Luther King Jr.*, ed. Clayborne Carson (Berkeley: University of California Press, 2007), 6:230.

4. Julissa Higgins, "Read George W. Bush's Speech at the Dallas Shooting Memorial Service," *Time*, July 12, 2016, http://time.com/4403510/george -w-bush-speech-dallas-shooting-memorial-service/.

5. See Heb. 11:1.

6. Ps. 1:3.

7. "Steven Curtis Chapman Chats about Grief, Hope, Trust, His New Book & Tour," YouTube video, posted by "Kay Wyma," April 12, 2017, https://www .youtube.com/watch?v=08N4mtgwVPc&t=901s.

8. Ps. 121:1–2, 5, 8.

9. Corrie ten Boom, *The Hiding Place* (New York: Bantam Books, 1974).

Chapter 10 Rather Than Be Overwhelmed by Bitterness, Be Overwhelmed by Forgiveness

1. Leon F. Seltzer, PhD, "Don't Let Your Anger 'Mature' into Bitterness," *Psychology Today*, January 14, 2015, https://www.psychologytoday.com/blog/evo lution-the-self/201501/don-t-let-your-anger-mature-bitterness.

2. David Sedley, "Video of Holocaust Survivor Forgiving Mengele Goes Viral," *Times of Israel*, October 1, 2017, https://www.timesofisrael.com/video -of-holocaust-survivor-forgiving-mengele-goes-viral/.

Chapter 11 Rather Than Be Overwhelmed by Present Sufferings, Be Overwhelmed by an Eternal Perspective

1. See Ps. 16:11.

2. Randy Alcorn, *In Light of Eternity* (New York: Waterbrook Press, 1999), 143.

3. See *Merriam-Webster Unabridged*, "joy," accessed March 1, 2018, https:// www.merriam-webster.com/dictionary/joy.

4. Anne Lamott, *Grace Eventually* (New York: Riverhead Books, 2007).

5. Janet Denison, "Seven Things You Won't Find in Heaven," *Janet Denison* (blog), January 30, 2018, https://www.janetdenison.org/blog/seven-things -you-wont-find-in-heaven/.

6. Shahesta Shaitly, "Living with Death," *Guardian,* June 18, 2011, https:// www.theguardian.com/lifeandstyle/2011/jun/19/living-death-terminal-illness -cancer.

Chapter 12 Rather Than Be Overwhelmed by *Any* Trappings of This World, Be Overwhelmed by Hope

1. John 19:30.
2. Mike Bird, "N. T. Wright: The Church Continues the Revolution Jesus Started," *Christianity Today*, October 13, 2016, http://www.christianitytoday .com/ct/2016/october-web-only/n-t-wright-jesus-death-does-more-than-just-get -us-into-heav.html.
3. See Heb. 11:1.
4. Isa. 43:1–3
5. Isa. 41:10.
6. Carolyn Weber, *Surprised by Oxford* (Nashville: Thomas Nelson, 2011).
7. Gen. 2:18.
8. Ps. 22:1
9. "Katherine Adams at Memphis NYWC," YouTube video, 2:34, from a speech at the National Youth Workers' Convention in Memphis on November 17, 2017, posted by "Paper for Water," January 12, 2018, https://www.youtube .com/watch?v=kWNKH3hkt2k.
10. Isa. 43:4.
11. Eph. 3:17–19.

Kay Wills Wyma, former White House staffer, international banker, and entrepreneur, is a mom of five who writes about seeing beyond life's pressures in order to navigate life and thrive together. She is the author of two books and blogs at the popular themoatblog.com. Kay also hosts a video podcast with friends called the SaySomething Show. She has been featured on *TODAY*, CNN, and *Focus on the Family*, and has contributed to the *NYT Motherlode*, *DMagazine*, *Thriving Families*, and more. Kay lives in Dallas, Texas, with her family. Connect with her at kaywyma.com.

CONNECT WITH KAY WYMA AT
TheMoatBlog.com

- -

f MOATblog   **◎** kaywyma

𝕏 @themoatblog   **▶** Kay Wyma